The Maserati 250F

CLASSIC COMPETITION CARS

The Maserati 250F

Anthony Pritchard

Aston Publications

Classic Competition Cars

THE MASERATI 250F

by Anthony Pritchard
Foreword by Roy Salvadori

ISBN 0-94662-03-7

Published by Aston Publications,
Bourne End House, Harvest Hill,
Bourne End, Bucks., SL8 5JJ
Telephone: 06285-25023

Sole distributor to the UK book trade:
Springfield Books Ltd., Springfield House,
Norman road, Denby Dale, Huddersfield,
West Yorkshire.
Telephone: 0484-864955

This first edition published in 1985 by
Aston Publications

Printed in the United Kingdom by
Plaistow Press Ltd., 3 New Plaistow Road,
Stratford, London, E15 3JA.

Front cover:
Juan Fangio (lightweight 250F)
in practice for the 1957 European
Grand Prix at Aintree.
(T. C. March)

Rear cover:
Upper: Roy Salvadori with the
Gilby Engineering car, 2507, in
the paddock at Silverstone, May
1954. (T. C. March)
Lower: Peter Collins with the
Owen Organization 250F, 2509,
in the 1955 British Grand Prix
at Aintree. (T. C. March)

Contents

Note: All black and white photographs by T. C. March in this publication are the copyright of Aston Publications. Full-plate prints of any black and white photograph by T. C. March in this book can be supplied at £3 each inclusive of VAT and postage. The publishers have a wide range of motor racing negatives covering the years 1950-1970. No catalogue is published and enquiries should be specific. Please address any enquiry to the publishers and enclose a stamped addressed envelope. Prints are supplied on the basis that they will not be reproduced without prior written consent and agreed reproduction fee.

Foreword by Roy Salvadori

My years in Formula 1 with Sid Greene's Gilby team were among the most satisfactory and successful in my racing career. When Sid told me in the autumn of 1953 that he proposed buying a new Maserati Grand Prix car, it was to prove for me a major turning point in my racing career. We travelled together to Modena to discuss the purchase with the Orsis and I had the opportunity of driving the 250F with which Juan Fangio had just won the Argentine Grand Prix in January 1954.

We took delivery of our car in April 1954. Although we suffered problems with the car in its early days, including rather alarming clutch weakness and a very high non-standard first gear, it was the one truly competitive Formula 1 car available to private entrants. We raced the car weekend after weekend for three successive seasons and I enjoyed considerable success in most British races. We also raced on a very limited financial budget, which meant that I always had to drive with great self-discipline to restrict the engine revs, but I think that the 250F and I were probably the most successful Formula 1 combination in British events during the years 1954 to 1956. In 1954 I won a total of three races with the 250F, finished second four times and was third on two occasions. Because of our limited budget, we were rarely able to race abroad, but we managed to take in the French Grand Prix, in which I retired after battling with the works Maseratis, and I finished third at Rouen, which was more than satisfying.

It was much the same story in 1955, when I won with the 250F in six races as well as finishing second to my friend Peter Collins with the Owen Organization 250F in the *Daily Express* International Trophy at Silverstone. By 1956 our 250F was out-dated compared with the works cars, but as well as continuing to enjoy considerable success in British races of a less important nature, I had the satisfaction of leading all the works cars from every team in the British Grand Prix at Silverstone before I retired with a minor mechanical problem, and overseas I managed to finish third in the Caen Grand Prix and set a lap record.

The 250F was a delightful car to race; it had all the shortcomings of Formula 1 cars of its era, vibration at speed and sheer physical hard work to race. It did, however, have superb handling with a slight trace of understeer, a very good power to weight ratio and very well spaced gear ratios. In addition, it was a reliable car that our team could run in race after race with a minimum of mechanical attention.

Pleasant though my memories are of the 250F, I cannot, of course, forget accidents with the car that included a crash in the Oulton Park Gold Cup in 1954 when the throttles jammed open and a rather nasty experience in the *Daily Express* Trophy at Silverstone in 1956 when the rear end locked up and the car rolled. But despite those accidents, my years with the 250F and the Gilby team were among the happiest in my racing career, working with a good team, supported by superb mechanics and driving for an entrant, Sid Greene, who put immense zest and enthusiasm into his racing.

My most vivid and unforgettable memory of a car being driven on, or even past, the limit was a 250F Maserati being thrown round the Nürburgring and Rouen circuits by Juan Fangio, both of which races he won. While undoubtedly Fangio was the fastest driver of the era, and probably of all time, he needed a forgiving car to make these feats possible, and that is exactly what the 250F was.

ROY SALVADORI
MONACO
August 1985

1. Background to Maserati

For much of Maserati's racing history, it was the familiar situation of 'always the bridesmaid and never the bride'. Throughout the thirties the products of the Maserati brothers in Bologna were overshadowed by the Scuderia Ferrari-entered Alfa Romeos and in the post-war years by Enzo Ferrari's own cars. When Mercedes-Benz were racing Grand Prix cars, between 1934 and 1939 and 1954-55, then both Italian teams were overshadowed.

There were six Maserati brothers but Carlo died in 1910 and Mario was more interested in artistic pursuits than the internal combustion engine. The mainstays of the Maserati factory were Ernesto, Bindo and Ettore. Alfieri died in 1932 following an operation.

Alfieri, Bindo and Ettore had all worked for Isotta-Fraschini and in 1922 Alfieri moved on to the Diatto organization. At Diatto, Alfieri developed a 3-litre version of a production car and the the 20S based on Diatto's 2-litre Model 20. The next step was a sleek, straight-eight 2-litre Grand Prix car which Alfieri produced in time for the 1925 Italian Grand Prix. Diatto were in fact in financial difficulties and Alfieri took over the project, which formed the basis of all straight-eight Maseratis until 1934. From 1926 onwards the small Maserati factory produced a successful line of firstly, straight-eight competition cars, and, from 1931, 4-cylinder cars. The straight-eight was developed into the very successful Tipo 8CM-3000, raced from 1933 onwards. In 1933 one of these cars was raced by the great Tazio Nuvolari, and his successes included wins in the Belgian Grand Prix, the Coppa Ciano and the Nice Grand Prix and second places at Pescara and Monza. Already Maserati were concentrating on exploiting the sale of competition cars to private owners, and buyers of the 8CM included Whitney Straight (who won the JCC International Trophy at Brooklands in 1934) and Phillipe Etancelin, who scored many successes in continental races.

In 1934 Maserati built a 6-cylinder 3.3-litre engine that was installed in the 8CM chassis and, in this form, was known as the Tipo 34. It was not a success, nor was the very ambitious V-8R1 car of 1935-36. It was, of course, competing at a time when racing was increasingly dominated by the German Mercedes-Benz and Auto Union teams. Likewise, the Tipo 8CTF developed for the 3000 cc supercharged/4500 cc

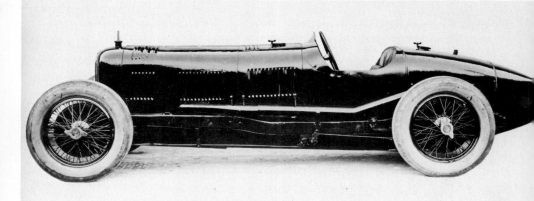

The 1925 Diatto 2-litre straight-eight Grand Prix car built by Fratelli Maserati and the direct forerunner of early Maseratis.

The 1930 Monaco Grand Prix with the field streaming up from Sainte Devote. No. 34 is Arcangeli's 2-litre straight-eight Maserati.

unsupercharged Grand Prix Formula proved a dismal failure in European events, but painstakingly prepared for Wilbur Shaw, one of these cars won at Indianapolis in 1939 and 1940.

During the thirties interest grew in 1500 cc supercharged cars for the *Voiturette* category, which was an area with immense potential for sales to private owners. It was a category which the British ERA team had joined in 1934 and in which Maserati introduced their Tipo 6CM with 6-cylinder twin overhead camshaft engine and independent front suspension in 1936. Maserati enjoyed immense success with the 6CM on the continental mainland, whilst ERA was equally successful in British events; when the two marques met, ERA was usually the winner.

In 1937, in an effort to match the performance of the British ERAs, Maserati produced the 4CM, which combined a more powerful 4-cylinder engine with the 6CM chassis. However, the competition in the category was becoming intense and in 1938 Alfa Romeo revealed their own *Voiturette*, the Tipo 158. Maserati responded in May 1939 with the 4CL with a four-valves-per-cylinder 1490 cc (78 x 78 mm) engine, but

Roy Salvadori competed with this elderly 4C-1500 4-cylinder Maserati during the 1948 sesson. He is seen here at Stanmer Park hill climb. (Guy Griffiths)

Whitney Straight with his 8CM-3000 Maserati at the International Trophy at Brooklands in 1934. In the beret standing by the cockpit is mechanic Giulio Ramponi.

The 4-cylinder twin overhead camshaft, twin-stage supercharged engine of the post-war 4CLT/48 Maserati. (Guy Griffiths)

both Maserati and Alfa Romeo were trounced by the new 1500 cc V-8 Mercedes-Benz W.165 cars in the Tripoli Grand Prix. It is not without significance (and indicates just how far Maserati had penetrated the *Voiturette* market) that 25 Maseratis were entered in this 1500 cc race.

Alberto Ascari drove this 4CLT/48 into second place in the 1948 British Grand Prix at Silverstone. (Guy Griffiths)

Bindo, Ettore and Ernesto Maserati photographed in later days when they were running the Osca company at Bologna.

Adolfo Orsi bought the Maserati company in 1938, his son Omer becoming managing director. The works were transferred from Bologna to Modena and the surviving Maserati brothers entered into a ten-year service agreement. They left at the end of 1947 to found their own new Osca company, which was to build a line of very successful 1100 cc and 1500 cc sports/racing cars and not-so-successful single-seaters.

In post-war days Maserati continued to rely on the 16-valve 4-cylinder car which was gradually developed. Twin-stage supercharging was adopted in 1947 and the tubular chassis 4CLT car appeared later that year. In 1948 came the 4CLT/48 or 'San Remo' (it first ran in the San Remo Grand Prix) with modified chassis, new coil spring front suspension and lower and neater bodywork.The post-war 4-cylinder cars were very popular with private owners, including Tazio Nuvolari, the Scuderia Milano, Scuderia Ambrosiana (undoubtetdly the most successful) and Swiss entrant Enrico Platé. Indeed, apart from the venerable ERAs, still favoured out of necessity by British drivers, and the lumbering 4.5-litre Lago-Talbots, the private entrant had very little alternative. Whilst the Maseratis scored innumerable successes in the late forties and early fifties in minor events, in major races the works Alfa Romeos and the new V-12 Ferraris were very much the dominant marques.

But while Modena continued to service and sell the old blown 4-cylinder cars, a new breed of Maserati was being developed.

Froilan Gonzalez and the twin-plug A6GCM in the pits at the 1952 Italian Grand Prix.

2. Background to the 250F

Before they left the company that they had founded, the Maseratis had been working on a 6-cylinder sports car engine, the A6 of 1488 cc (66 x 72.5 mm) and with much in common with the pre-war 6CM engine. This new engine had been bench-tested as early as 1945, but the complete car did not appear until 1947. From this basic design Maserati developed the A6GCS 1978 cc sports/racing car. In 1951 development took a major step forward when Alberto Massimino started work on a new and much more advanced 6-cylinder engine of 1988 cc (75 x 75 mm) with light alloy construction throughout, twin overhead camshafts and, with single-plug ignition and three twin-choke Weber carburettors, a power output of around 165 bhp. This engine, with a 4-speed Maserati gearbox, was installed in a simple, well-braced tubular steel chassis with double wishbone and coil spring front suspension and a rigid rear axle suspended on quarter-elliptic springs. The simple monoposto body followed the lines of the 'San Remo', but was lower with a longer nose cowling.

Throughout 1952 these cars, typed the A6GCM, were raced on a rather half-hearted basis by the works, and with two cars running under the banner of the Brazilian team, Escuderia Bandeirantes. At the Autodrome Grand Prix at Monza in June a team of three works cars was entered. One was driven by Juan Fangio, who had driven to Monza from Paris after competing the previous day with the V-16 BRM in the Ulster Trophy. After starting from the back of the grid, the Argentinian, trying hard to make up ground, crashed badly at Lesmo and suffered injuries that put him out of racing for the rest of the year.

It was not until the 1952 Italian Grand Prix that the A6GCM showed any real signs of being competitive. At Monza the Maserati factory entered a new twin-plug car developing some 177 bhp for Froilan Gonzalez. The A6GCM's fuel tank was too small for Gonzalez to run through the race without a pit stop, but he led for the first 37 laps and rejoined the race to finish second to Ascari's Ferrari. Other twin-plug cars were driven by Felice Bonetto (fifth) and Franco Rol (who retired). Another hard-fought second place for Gonzalez followed a week later in the Modena Grand Prix.

In the 1953 British Grand Prix this A6GCM was driven into second place by Juan Fangio. (T. C. March)

15

For 1953 Maserati embarked on a full season of racing with A6GCMs. Since 1952 World Championship events had been held to 2000 cc unsupercharged Formula 2 regulations (because there were insufficient competitive Formula 1 cars) and this was to be the last season before the new 2500 cc unsupercharged Grand Prix Formula came into force at the beginning of 1954. The A6GCMs were much modified; engine dimensions were revised to 76.2 x 72 mm (1997 cc), power output had increased to something over 180 bhp, the chassis was stiffened and there was a new lower and sleeker body. With a strong team of drivers consisting of Fangio, Gonzalez and Bonetto, together with Marimon running in Argentinian blue and yellow colours and de Graffenried driving a private car for Swiss entrant Enrico Platé, Maserati was able to offer a stiff challenge to Ferrari, who had dominated the 1952 season.

Throughout the year Fangio battled hard to get to grips with the Ferrari team, finishing second in the French Grand Prix, after one of the closest battles in motor racing history, to young Mike Hawthorn at the wheel of a Ferrari, second in the British Grand Prix and second in the German race. Fangio managed to win at Monza after another race-long battle, but only after Ascari had spun twice at the last corner of the race.

Emmanuel de Graffenried with his A6GCM laps the older 1952 A6GCM of Francesco Landi in the 1953 Italian Grand Prix. (LAT)

Directly developed from the 1953 A6GCM was the 250F (originally known as the 250/F1). A great deal of development work was carried out on the engine, which had a capacity of 2493 cc (84 x 75 mm) and claimed to develop 240 bhp at 7400 rpm running on a mixture of methanol and benzol. There was a new multi-tubular 'space-frame' chassis with light tubular structure to carry the body, new suspension by double wishbones and coil springs at the front and, at the rear, a de Dion axle and transverse leaf spring. This de Dion axle, located vertically by a ball guide running in a sliding channel and fore and aft by twin radius rods, and with the tube running in front of the final drive, was copied from the layout seen on the Tipo 553 Ferraris that had first run in the Italian Grand Prix in September 1953. The 4-speed gearbox was mounted in unit with and to the right of the final drive. The aluminium body was superbly styled and characterized by the heavy louvring and the reverse slope of the air intake.

The 250F was first tested at the Modena Autodrome in December 1953 and raced in the Argentine the following month. Although it was plagued by many early problems, including oil overheating and frothing, a week clutch and breakage of the de Dion tube, it was clear that the 250F, which was the work of engineers Colombo, Bellentani and Alfieri, had been superbly conceived and that its potential was immense.

3. 1954: Dawn of a New Era in Racing

After the 1953 Italian Grand Prix, Officine Alfieri Maserati held a test session at the Monza Autodrome at which selected drivers were invited to try a couple of laps at the wheel of the A6GCM that had finished seventh in the race shared by Mantovani and Musso. It was part of an active sales campaign for the 1954 250F by the Orsis, and drivers to handle the car included Johnny Claes, John Fitch, Louis Rosier, Harry Schell, Roy Salvadori and Maurice Trintignant. It was believed that Trintignant was being given a trial as a possible member of the works team and that both Salvadori and Wharton were to drive 250Fs for private entrants.

The 250F was the one serious Formula 1 contender available to private entrants. The only other constructor interested in selling cars was Connaught, whose B-series car was not ready until 1955 and who, in any case, had no successful track record other than minor wins with their underpowered A-series Formula 2 cars. Ferrari was not interested in private sales, but Maranello did update and re-engine Formula 2 cars for Reg Parnell and Louis Rosier. The result was a string of orders for the 250F from Roberto Mieres, Harry Schell, 'B. Bira', Gilby Engineering (for Salvadori to drive), Stirling Moss and the Owen Organization (for Ken Wharton to drive). The first delivery of a new 250F was Gilby's British Racing Green-painted car, chassis number 2507, in April, followed by the Moss car, 2508, painted light green, in May, the 'B. Bira' car, 2504, in June and the Owen car, 2509, in July. In the meanwhile

Roy Salvadori with the Gilby Engineering 250F, 2507, in the paddock at the *Daily Express* **trophy at Silverstone. At Silverstone this 250F was plagued by mechanical problems. (T. C. March)**

Mieres, Schell and 'B. Bira' were supplied with interim 1953-54 cars, consisting of the 1953 A6GCM chassis and the latest 2500 cc engine. In addition A6GCMs fitted with 250F engines were supplied to Emmanuel de Graffenried and Jorge Daponte. The 250F engine fitted neatly in the 1953 chassis, but the handling left much to be desired and the rigid rear axle of the A6GCM was not really up to taking the power of the 250 engine.

Originally Maserati had not planned to race a works team, but a change of mind was made at a fairly late stage, and it was this decision that delayed the delivery of new cars. Maserati's works team consisted of Fangio, Marimon, Musso and Mantovani, but it was not an entirely satisfactory arrangement; Fangio was to drive for Maserati only until the new Mercedes-Benz W.196 was ready to race, and Maserati did not achieve a settled team for much of the season.

A view of the induction side of the engine of the 1954 250F. (T. C. March)

Throughout 1954 racing was, in minor events, a repetition of 1953, closely fought rivalry between Maserati and Ferrari, who was racing 4-cylinder cars: these were the Tipo 625, first seen as long ago as 1951 and, engine size apart, virtually identical to the 1952-53 Formula 2 Ferraris, and the Tipo 553 'Squalo', with multi-tubular chassis and pannier fuel tanks, first seen in 2-litre prototype form at the 1953 Italian Grand Prix. This all changed when the new straight-eight Mercedes-Benz W.196 made its debut in the French Grand Prix on the Reims circuit in July and won first time out in the hands of Fangio. Thereafter both Italian teams were struggling to beat Mercedes efficiency and sophistication and Fangio and Mercedes, although not without problems, dominated the World Championship. As for other contenders, Gordini, racing on almost non-existent finance, was still struggling with his outdated 6-cylinder cars, the Jano-designed Lancia D.50 V-8 cars promised an appearance all season, but only made it at the last race, the Vanwall was still very much in the early stages of development and none of the other British teams had yet put their act together.

In December 1953 there was a frantic rush to get the Maseratis ready for shipping on 26 December to the first race of the 1954 season, the Argentine Grand

Prix. The prototype 250F was badly damaged at Modena Autodrome, when a sports Maserati spun into it while it was parked in front of the pits and the Maserati staff worked through Christmas Day to repair it. Two new 250Fs and two interim cars were sent to Buenos Aires and faced immediate problems in practice. Testing at Modena had not prepared the cars for the high temperatures of the South American summer and the engines were overheating badly, Maserati attempted to solve this by cutting large holes in the noses of the cars to improve air flow. Another problem was oil frothing, which resulted in bearing failure, and as a temporary expedient Bertocchi bought all the fresh olive oil that he could find and mixed this with the engine oil. The cars were also handling far from well, apparently because the chassis frames were too stiff, but this problem was solved by cutting away two diagonal bracing tubes in the cockpit.

The Argentine Grand Prix was run as a three-hour event on the Buenos Aires Autodrome and the first hour was dominated by the Ferraris with Fangio in fourth place, but heavy rain and a drop in temperature transformed the race. Fangio stopped at the pits for a set of hastily cut anchorized rain tyres to be fitted, and Ferrari team manager Nello Ugolini lodged a protest on the grounds that five instead of the permitted three mechanics had worked on Fangio's car. On the assumption that his protest would be upheld, he slowed off the works Ferraris and Fangio sailed into the lead and an easy victory, the protest being rejected. The interim cars of Schell, 'B. Bira' and de Graffenried finished sixth, seventh and eighth. A fortnight later Fangio drove a 250F in the Formule Libre Buenos Aires City Grand Prix, but retired because of rear axle problems. The race was won by Trintignant with an Ecurie Rosier Ferrari, but Mieres took an excellent second place with his interim A6GCM/250F car.

Stirling Moss finished third in his heat with 2508 at the *Daily Express* **Trophy, but retired in the final because of a broken de Dion tube. (T. C. March)**

Back in Europe there were a number of minor races before the next *Grande Epreuve*. At Siracusa, Mantovani finished third behind the Ferraris of Farina and Trintignant (the latter, following his success at Buenos Aires, was now a member of Scuderia Ferrari) and at Pau on Easter Monday Marimon with the sole works Maserati entered retired with failure of the de Dion axle, probably the result of damage caused when he was rammed on the grid by Farina's Ferrari. The same day Salvadori drove the Gilby car on its debut at Goodwood. After taking second place to Parnell's Ferrari in the 7-lap Lavant Cup, Salvadori faced Wharton with the V-16 BRM in the Richmond Trophy. The BRM was faster on the straights, but Salvadori was closing up on braking and pushing Wharton through the corners. Wharton was one of the hardest drivers, and there was no prospect of him letting Salvadori by, and on lap 19 the two cars collided and spun at Lavant. Both cars rejoined the race, but a lap later Salvadori was out; the Maserati's clutch had exploded with such force that pieces of clutch punched holes through the 250F's bodywork.

Four days before the Bordeaux Grand Prix, Stirling Moss was testing his new car, financed largely by BP, at Modena and there was a frantic rush to get it to the French race. Stirling drove cautiously to finish fourth behind a trio of works Ferraris. Both Moss and Salvadori were entered in the *Daily Express* Trophy at Silverstone in May, an important race in the British calendar run in two qualifying heats and a final. Froilan Gonzalez won his heat for Ferrari with a Tipo 553 'Squalo' car and took over Trintignant's 625 to win the final. Moss was holding second place in the final when the 250F's de Dion axle failed (a persistent weakness on these cars in 1954) and Salvadori, who was second in his heat, finished tenth in the final after a pit stop for work on the throttle linkage. On the Moss car a stronger de Dion tube made in Britain was substituted. The following weekend Marimon finished fourth in the Bari Grand Prix on the Lungomare circuit after stops to take on extra water and fuel, and at the end of May Moss won the inaugural Formule Libre '200' race on the Aintree circuit.

On 6 June Maserati scored wins in two minor events. In the Rome Grand Prix on the fast Castelfusano circuit works cars were driven by Marimon, Mantovani and Musso and Moss entered his private car. Marimon led for most of the race to win from Schell (with his interim car) and Mantovani. Immediately after the finish the oil tank split on Marimon's car. Oil seemed to be Maserati's biggest problem in 1954 and the 250Fs were plagued by oil problems, much of it due to the effect of engine vibration on rigidly mounted pipes. Moss had held a comfortable, smooth second

At Spa-Franchorchamps Juan Fangio scored his second win for Maserati with 2505. (LAT)

For Stirling it was the same story in the British Grand Prix as at Silverstone in May. He again worked his way up to second place only to retire because of a broken de Dion tube. (T. C. March)

place until he suffered transmmission trouble shortly before the finish and he pushed the car across the line into sixth place. The same day 'B. Bira' drove his interim car in the Grand Prix des Frontières at Chimay; there were only nine starters and he won easily from Pilette's Gordini. The same weekend Salvadori won two short races at Snetterton and finished second in two at Goodwood.

By the Belgian Grand Prix at Spa-Francorchamps on 20th June, Maserati had made a number of changes to the works 250Fs, including the introduction of a strengthened de Dion tube and a new cylinder head with larger inlet valves, new camshafts and strengthened con-rods. Works 250Fs were driven by Fangio (who had not competed since the Argentine races), Marimon and Mantovani, while private cars were driven by Moss and 'B. Bira' (who had just taken delivery of his 250F). Mieres had his usual interim car. Facing the Maseratis were four works Ferraris. At the end of the first day's practice, in the cool of the evening, Fangio turned in a fantastic lap of 4 min 22.1 sec, taking pole position and matching the outright circuit record, which he had set in the 1951 race with a supercharged Alfa Romeo 159. To achieve this Fangio had taken the 250F up to 8100 rpm (the maximum permitted limit on the works cars was now 8200 rpm, whilst private owners were still limited to 7400 rpm) and back at the pits the 250F was leaking oil from just about every joint, the brakes were red hot and the car shimmered in a haze of heat. Fangio made a poor start in the race, but took the lead on lap three to win from Trintignant and Moss. In the closing laps Fangio's 250F was grounding its tail on the bumpier parts of the circuit because the rear leaf spring had settled and it was trailing its fuel-retaining strap.

Although Maserati had won the first two Championship races of the year, it was now that the team's problems started in earnest. A fortnight later the Mercedes-Benz W.196 *Stromlinienwagen* driven by Fangio, Kling and Herrmann made their debut at Reims and Maserati had lost their top driver. Arrangements were made with Gianni Lancia for Alberto Ascari (1952 and 1953 World Champion) and Luigi Villoresi, both of whom were contracted to drive the new Lancia D.50 when it was ready, to handle 250Fs at Reims and a third car was entered. Maserati had made an offer to Moss that if he drove as hard as he liked and broke the engine of his 250F, they would replace it free of charge. Moss was unable to drive in the French Grand Prix as he was contracted to appear for Jaguar in the Reims 12 Hours race, which immediately preceded it, so Maserati borrowed his 250F for Villoresi to drive. Private 250Fs were driven by 'B. Bira', Roy Salvadori (making a rare continental appearance with the Gilby 250F) and Ken Wharton (the Owen Organization had just taken delivery of their car, which was to be used for testing and something to race until the new BRM was ready).

The race was dominated by the Mercedes, and Fangio and Kling took the first two places. All three works Ferraris blew their engines, and Ascari blew up the engine of his 250F on the first lap. Third place went to Manzon's private Ferrari and the sole Maserati finishers were 'B. Bira' and Villoresi in fourth and fifth places. The following weekend 'B. Bira' and Salvadori finished second and third behind Trintignant's Ferrari in the Rouen Grand Prix. It was on the way back from this race that Mieres's A6GCM/250F was wrecked when the transporter crashed and the Argentinian was so fed up with it that he did not bother to have it rebuilt.

The Maserati team missed practice for the British Grand Prix at Silverstone because the transporters had gone to the wrong port. When the cars did arrive at the circuit, it was only too evident that they had been hastily prepared and the mechanics had to work through the night, supported and assisted by Moss's cool and able

Third place in the British Grand Prix was taken by Onofre Marimon with 2506. (T. C. March)

In twelfth place at the British Grand Prix came Harry Schell with his interim car, 2503.
(T. C. March)

mechanic, Alf Francis. A special practice session was laid on for the works Maseratis, but this did not count for grid positions and they had to start from the back. The works cars were driven by Ascari, Villoresi and Marimon, while private 250Fs were driven by Moss, Salvadori, Wharton and 'B. Bira'.

At Silverstone the streamlined Mercedes proved a complete handful and the race settled down to the Ferraris of Gonzalez and Hawthorn leading from Fangio and Moss. Stirling was in tremendous form, passing, on lap 55, Fangio's Mercedes, which was battered from contact with the oil drums lining Silverstone, jumping out of gear and spraying the driver with oil, and three laps later slipping past Hawthorn. Only ten laps from the finish Moss was out of the race because of a broken de Dion tube and the Ferraris of Gonzalez and Hawthorn took the first two places ahead of Marimon, who had driven the best race of his career. Ascari lost two minutes in the pits complaining about the steering of his 250F, rejoined the race, blew up the engine and then took over Villoresi's car — which he also blew up! A week later Moss finished second to Trintignant's works Ferrari in the Caen Grand Prix.

By the German Grand Prix Moss and his Maserati had been invited to join the works team and 2508 appeared at the Nürburgring hastily repainted red but retaining a green nose-band. Other works cars were to be driven by Villoresi, Mantovani and Mieres. Mantovani was at the wheel of his own brand new car, 2511. The three works cars proper of Villoresi, Marimon and Mieres all featured the oil tank mounted in the tail instead of below the carburettors. This eliminated oil frothing and was a modification later carried out on all 250Fs.

It was a bad race for Maserati. During the second day of practice Onofre Marimon lost control just before the Wehrseifen bridge — about six miles after the start/finish line — and suffered injuries from which he died within minutes. Thirty-year-old Marimon was a ragged, rather erratic driver during 1953 and the early part of 1954, but recently his driving had become steadier and more consistent. He was

Ken Wharton in the British race with the Owen Organization car, 2509. (T. C. March)

immensely popular with other drivers and his fellow-Argentinians were particularly affected by his death. The works Maserati team withdrew from the race, but Moss, Mieres and Mantovani all decided to run as private entrants.

For this race Mercedes had revealed their open-wheel version of the W.196, and Fangio scored yet another convincing victory from the Ferraris of Gonzalez/Hawthorn and Trintignant. Moss held third place at the start of the race and seemed ready to have a go with the leaders when big-end failure put him out of the race. Mieres retired a lap later because of a leaking fuel tank, but Mantovani, a very steady and reliable driver by Italian standards, drove a smooth race to finish fifth behind Kling's Mercedes.

For the *Daily Dispatch* meeting at Oulton Park the following weekend, Moss was unable to drive his own car as it was still being repaired after the German race and drove the works 250F, 2506, that Villoresi should have driven at the Nürburgring. He started from the back of the grid after missing practice and slashed through the field to win the Gold Cup race from Parnell's Ferrari and the Formule Libre event from Gerard's Cooper-Bristol. Roy Salvadori was holding second place in the Formula 1 Gold Cup race when the throttle jammed open. He pushed the two cut-out switches that Gilby had fitted to be able to test the magnetos individually, but in fact operated only one of them and the 250F went off the road and hit a tree. Roy escaped with bruising, but the 250F had to be sent back to Modena for a rebuild. The cause of the problem was that the engine had swallowed a valve and the valve head went through one of the carburettors and jammed the butterfly. The following weekend Moss with his private car was leading the circuit of Pescara, but was eliminated by a broken oil pipe feeding the gearbox. Musso won the race with his works car from 'B. Bira'.

Onofre Marimon who was tragically killed in practice for the German Grand Prix. (Publifoto)

Maserati entered four cars at the Swiss Grand Prix on the Bremgarten circuit for Moss, Mieres (who was at the wheel of his own new car), Mantovani and Schell (having his first drive with the 250F as opposed to the interim car). Moss's car was always fitted with a right-hand accelerator (instead of the usual central accelerator of the 250F) and at this race Schell's car was similarly fitted so that there was a spare for the new team leader. A fifth private Maserati was the Owen car driven by Ken Wharton; since the British Grand Prix this had been extensively modified by the fitting of Dunlop magnesium-alloy disc wheels, Dunlop disc brakes, shorter exhaust tail-pipes and the transfer of the oil tank from below the carburettors to alongside the driver. Both Moss and Schell were eliminated by loss of oil pressure and the finishing order was Fangio (Mercedes), Gonzalez (Ferrari) and Herrmann (Mercedes) in the first three places. The Maseratis of Mieres, Mantovani and Wharton finished fourth, fifth and sixth.

For the Italian Grand Prix at Monza both Italian teams threw the maximum effort into this race on home territory. Maserati entered cars for Moss (at the wheel of 2508), Villoresi, Mantovani, Musso and Mieres (all the last three were at the wheel of their own cars), while a sixth 250F, hastily repainted blue, was entered for Louis Rosier, who was buying an ex-works car at the end of the year; when this blew its engine in practice, another 250F, still painted red, was hastily substituted. During practice Musso's car was fitted with a modified exhaust, with the two three-branch manifolds feeding into a single large-bore tail-pipe (instead of the usual twin tail-pipes). Later in practice this was transferred to Villoresi's car, but it was not used in the race. Ferrari entered a total of six cars and streamlined Mercedes were driven by both Fangio and Kling.

Stirling Moss, by now a member of the works team, drove 2508 with the latest, more powerful engine in the Italian Grand Prix. It was his best race to that time and he was leading when an oil pipe broke. (Publifoto)

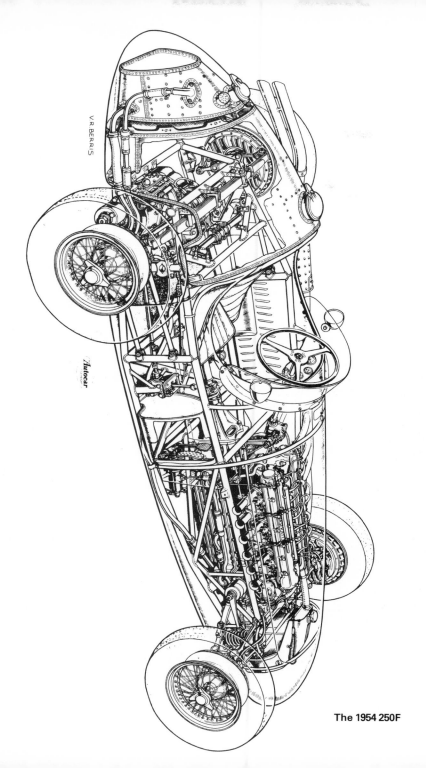

V R BERRIS

Autocar

The 1954 250F

In practice Moss was third fastest, three-tenths of a second slower than pole positon man Fangio, and after a gentle start Villoresi and Moss moved up to hold third and fourth places behind Ascari (Ferrari) and Fangio. Villoresi, who had turned in his best performance for a couple of years, over-revved and broke the 250F engine, Moss passed Ascari to take the lead, Ascari fought back, went ahead again and retired two laps later with a broken valve.

For the first time in his racing career Stirling was leading a *Grande Epreuve* and with 12 laps to go held a 20-second lead. Three laps later Moss was in the pits because the oil pressure was dropping on corners; the tank was topped up and he rejoined the race in second palce behind Fangio. It was to no avail because the suction pipe from the rear-mounted oil tank had broken, air was sucked into the lubrication system and the bearings were ruined. Shortly afterwards Moss stopped ready to push the car across the line at the finish of the race. Mantovani had worked his way through to battle for second place with Hawthorn, only to fall back and coast to the finish after the de Dion tube broke.

Fangio went on to win his sixth Championship race victory of the year and the only Maserati drivers to appear in the results were Mantovani ninth and Moss tenth. Moss was generally regarded as the moral victor of the race, but it was a poor consolation for him and for Maserati, who had tried so hard to get the cars properly sorted and had started the race with such high hopes.

There were a number of minor events before the final round of the World Championship at Barcelona and two of the most interesting were the British races at Goodwood and Aintree. In the Goodwood Trophy on the Sussex circuit Moss drove a good race to win from Collins (with the new 2500 cc version of the 'Vanwall Special') and Salvadori. In the Formule Libre race Moss was third behind Collins (Ferrari 4.5-litre 'Thinwall Special') and Wharton (V-16 BRM), but enjoyed a fine scrap with Hawthorn with the Vanwall Special, who finished only a couple of yards behind in fourth place.

It was a battle that was repeated in the *Daily Telegraph* Trophy at Aintree the following weekend. Here Moss sailed away into the lead and Mike had to fight hard to hold off Schell's Maserati, which finished a bare second behind the British car. Moss also won the Formule Libre race at Aintree with Mantovani in second place.

At the Spanish Grand Prix on the Pedralbes street circuit Maserati entered cars for Moss, Mantovani, Mieres, Musso, Schell and, provided that it was not needed by the works, a brand new car, 2501, for Spanish driver Francesco Godia-Sales. The new car had been exhibited at the Paris Salon and apart from incorporating all the year's mechanical developments had new and smoother bodywork. Opposition came from the usual strong teams of Ferraris and Mercedes, but in addition the new Lancia D.50s were making their race debut in the hands of Ascari and Villoresi.

Harry Schell had agreed with the Maserati team manager to start the race with half-full tanks and act as the 'hare'. Both Ascari and Villoresi retired their Lancias early in the race, Moss was eliminated by oil scavenge pump failure on lap 20, but Schell battled for the lead with Hawthorn's 'Squalo' Ferrari until he spun, dented the tail and dropped back to fourth place; he retired not long afterwards with gearbox trouble. Hawthorn went on to score a fine victory for Ferrari from Musso and Fangio, who had never been able to challenge for the lead and whose Mercedes sounded and looked sicker and sicker as the race progressed.

It was an encouraging end to the year for Maserati, who believed that they could look forward to 1955 with a well-developed car and a strong team of drivers, headed by Moss and backed up by Musso and Mantovani.

4. 1955: Success is Limited

For the second season in succession Maserati prospects in the World Championship were dashed. The team had always felt a little bitter about the loss of Fangio to Mercedes-Benz in 1954 and now Mercedes persuaded Moss to join their team. As a replacement team leader Maserati signed up French driver Jean Behra, determined and able and a member of the Gordini équipe for three years; unfortunately despite his many qualities Behra was no Moss. The team was completed by Musso, Mantovani and Mieres, all fast, reliable drivers, but not in the World Championship class. In a year dominated by Mercedes-Benz, the Maserati team was very much an also-ran. Ferrari was in much the same position, racing improved versions of the 1954 cars but with a rather stronger team of drivers. At the start of the season Lancia looked the most likely Italian prospect. The new Connaught first appeared at the Easter Goodwood meeting, but made only one continental appearance at the end of the year; Vanwall had a strong team consisting of Hawthorn and Schell, but it soon became evident that these British cars needed much more development work; and the new BRM did not race until the end of the year.

Changes to the 250F for 1955 were few. All the works cars had bodywork without louvres (as on the 250F raced by Godia-Sales at Barcelona in 1954); there were new brakes with wider drums (and greater lining area); a 5-speed gearbox was introduced and the single large-bore exhaust tail-pipe tried in practice at Monza in 1954 was used initially at some circuits, but later became standard wear.

The gear-change of the 5-speed gearbox fitted to 250Fs from 1955 onwards. (LAT)

Luigi Musso drove a fine race in the British Grand Prix at Aintree, finishing fifth behind the four Mercedes-Benz W.196 entries. (T. C. March)

The most significant modifications to a 250F were carried out to Stirling Moss's private car, which he had retained to run in non-Championship events and loaned to other drivers. The Moss car was fitted with SU fuel injection, a system which Moss had used with some success on his Cooper-Alta at Monza in 1953. In its 1954 form, running on three 42 mm Weber carburettors and fuel containing 50 per cent methanol, this 250F engine developed 215 bhp at 7000 rpm (so much for Maserati's claimed figures!), but with the same fuel and SU fuel injection, power output was boosted to 232 bhp at 7200 rpm. The price was a power loss between 4500 and 6000 rpm, which affected acceleration, and the system could not be regarded as completely successful. Other modifications to this car were the fitting of Dunlop magnesium-alloy wheels and disc brakes (as used on the Owen Organization car) with the booster pump mounted on the left-hand side of the gearbox and driven off the primary shaft.

Making a reputation for himself; Peter Collins's fine drives with the Owen Organization 250F led to an invitation to join Scuderia Ferrari in 1956. Collins is seen in the 1955 British Grand Prix in which he ran well until eliminated by clutch trouble. (Geoffrey Goddard)

At the beginning of the year 'B. Bira' ran his 250F in the 204-mile Formule Libre New Zealand Grand Prix at Ardmore and won from the 3-litre Ferraris of Peter Whitehead and Tony Gaze. This was the Siamese Prince's last win with his blue and yellow car before retiring from racing at the end of May. Eight days later the works team competed in the Argentine Grand Prix, a race run in the most appallingly torrid conditions with so many driver swaps during the race that, so far as the Ferrari team was concerned, it was not and is still not certain exactly which drivers drove what cars during the race. The only two drivers to run through the race without a break were local men Fangio, who won for Mercedes, and Mieres, who was delayed by a faulty fuel pump and finished fifth. The other works 250Fs driven by Schell/Behra and Musso/Mantovani were classified sixth and seventh. In the Formule Libre Buenos Aires City Grand Prix held a fortnight later the Mercedes dominated the results and the works Maseratis were right out of the picture: Behra finished fifth, local driver Menditeguy sixth, Schell seventh and Mantovani eighth.

In the usual early season European Formula 1 races the 250F achieved a fair measure of success. Mieres finished second in the Turin Grand Prix at Valentino Park to Ascari's Lancia, but it was a bad race for the Maserati team. Mantovani crashed heavily in practice, as a result of which he had a leg amputated above the knee. This charming and able driver's career was at an end, although he later tried a comeback in sports car racing without any luck. Maserati did not replace Mantovani, but gave young Cesare Perdisa a drive in a couple of races. At Pau on Easter Monday, Behra won from Castellotti's Lancia and the same day Salvadori won the Richmond Trophy at Goodwood after Moss had retired his 250F with fuel injection problems. At Bordeaux later in April the 250Fs of Behra, Musso and Mieres took the first three places, but the star of the race was Moss with his private car; with the 250F running on Webers again, Moss had a troubled race, plagued by brake troubles, forced to stop at the pits for a broken tank-retaining strap to be replaced by wire, but regaining two laps on the leaders and setting a new lap record in his chase back through the field to finish fourth.

Lance Macklin with the bizarrely painted Moss 250F in the 1954 British Grand Prix. It was an unhappy race for him. He finished eighth and last, eleven laps behind the winnner after spinning off and walking back to the pits to get help to restart the car. (T. C. March)

At Silverstone on 7 May all the leading private Maseratis met up with the new streamlined B-series Connaughts and the Vanwalls in the *Daily Express* Trophy. This race was at the height of its fame and although there were no continental works entries apart from Gordini, the Maserati drivers included Moss, Salvadori, Collins (with the Owen Organization car) and 'B. Bira'. In the opening laps Salvadori and Collins led from Fairman (Connaught), Hawthorn (Vanwall), Moss and McAlpine (Connaught). Moss retired early in the race, the British cars fell by the wayside and Collins took the lead to win from Salvadori and 'B. Bira'. The following day the works team ran in the Naples Ground Prix on the Posillipo road circuit. Ascari led throughout with his Lancia, but Musso and Behra took second and fourth places.

The first European *Grande Epreuve* was Monaco, last held as a race for single-seaters in 1951. In the face of immensely strong entries from Mercedes-Benz, Lancia and Ferrari, the prospects of success for the works 250Fs driven by Behra, Mieres, Musso and Perdisa were slim. Private entries came from Rosier and the Moss team, whose car was to be driven by Stirling's old HWM team-mate Lance Macklin; unfortunately Macklin was not fast enough to qualify as a starter. All three Mercedes retired, Ascari assumed the lead when Moss's leading Mercedes broke its engine and on the same lap locked a brake and crashed through the straw bales and sandbags into Monte Carlo harbour. Trintignant scored a surprise victory for Ferrari from Castellotti's Lancia. Three of the Maseratis retired and Perdisa, who had swapped cars with Behra when the team leader's engine began to run rough, took an unexpected third place.

Exactly the same Maserati entries appeared at the Belgian Grand Prix, four works cars and the private cars of Rosier and Moss. The Moss car was to be driven by Belgian band leader Johnny Claes, but non-started after the engine broke in practice. Among the opposition the most significant change was the appearance of only one Lancia for Castellotti; at the end of May Ascari had been killed at the wheel of a sports/racing Ferrari at Monza and Lancia, shocked by his death and already in financial trouble, were proposing to withdraw from racing. The race was dominated by the Mercedes of Fangio and Moss, and the 250Fs were never in serious contention for the lead. In the opening laps Behra battled for fourth place with Kling's slower Mercedes and two of the Ferrari team, but lost control on lap four on the left-hand bend before the final hairpin, bounced from bank to bank and abandoned the wrecked 250F in the ditch. He returned to the pits on foot to take over Mieres's car and finished fifth, whilst Musso took seventh place and Perdisa, still learning the circuit, was a poor eighth.

On 12 June there occurred the terrible Le Mans disaster which cost the lives of more than 80 spectators, and this resulted in the cancellation of the French, German, Swiss and Spanish Grands Prix. A week after the Le Mans race was the Dutch Grand Prix, in which Maserati entered three 250Fs for Behra, Mieres and Musso. Among the private Maserati entries were Horace Gould, running in his first World Championship race with the ex-'B. Bira' car still painted blue and yellow, and Peter Walker at the wheel of Moss's car. The race proved to be another Mercedes demonstration with Fangio and Moss taking the first two places, but Musso finished third and Mieres fourth (the Argentinian also set a new lap record of 92.96 mph); Behra, still groggy after he had been knocked down in the pit road at Le Mans the previous weekend, was sixth after a pit stop to complain about the rear suspension.

There were eight Maserati entries in the British Grand Prix, held for the first time on the flat, characterless, medium-speed Aintree circuit. Works cars were driven by Behra, Musso, Mieres and Simon, while the four private entries all came from British teams for Salvadori, Collins, Gould and Lance Macklin (the last-named at the wheel of the Moss car, which was now an unattractive grey). Moss and Fangio

Behra on the banking at Monza with the streamlined 250F. Following is Villoresi's Maserati. (Publifoto)

were fastest in practice with their Mercedes, but they were joined on the front row of the grid by Behra, and there were hopes that on this circuit he would be able to mix it for the lead. The race proved a complete Mercedes-Benz procession with the German cars in the first four places. Behra was third ahead of Kling until he blew his engine on lap 10, and Mieres also retired with engine failure. Simon went out with gear-selector problems. The sole works Maserati driver to finish was Musso in fifth place, after having led Taruffi's fourth-placed Mercedes for much of the race. Of the privateers the only finisher was Macklin in eighth position, eleven laps behind the winner.

Luigi Musso in the 1955 Italian Grand Prix with the standard 250F that he worked up to sixth place before retiring with gearbox trouble. For this race the 250Fs were fitted with deeper, more aerodynamic windscreens.

In minor British races the 250Fs were well to the fore. On 30 July, the Saturday of the Bank Holiday weekend, Mike Hawthorn had a go at the wheel of the Moss car and won the International Trophy at Crystal Palace from Schell's Vanwall. In August, Bob Gerard, normally seen at the wheel of an elderly but swift Cooper-Bristol, was given a drive with the Moss 250F at the Scottish Charterhall circuit and won the *Daily Record* Trophy from other 250Fs driven by Gould and Rosier. Salvadori was the victor in September in the *Daily Telegraph* Trophy at Aintree, but only after Reg Parnell's works Connaught had retired on the penultimate lap. The *Daily Express* had pioneered the post-war sponsorship of motor racing and by the mid-fifties most of the more popular newspapers were after a piece of the action.

By the Italian Grand Prix, held on the rebuilt road and banked track circuit at Monza, the entire Lancia équipe had been handed over to Ferrari, but because of tyre trouble in practice with the D50s, Maranello was forced to rely on the familiar Tipo 555 'Super-Squalo' cars. Mercedes-Benz entered two streamlined cars and two with exposed-wheel bodywork. Modena responded with an entry of five cars that included a new streamlined model driven by Behra; this car, 2518, was basically a standard 250F with full-width nose and tail sections and streamlined pontoons between the front and rear wheels. Normal 250Fs were driven by Musso, Mieres, Menditeguy and the young British driver Peter Collins, whom Maserati were thinking of signing up for 1956 (in fact he joined Ferrari). In addition Maserati loaned a works car to Horace Gould.

Musso in the pits at Monza. (Publifoto)

Maserati's greatest disappointment was that the streamlined 250F was not as quick as expected and Behra was only fifth fastest in practice. Once again the race was Mercedes-dominated, but two of the German cars retired, Castellotti finished third for Ferrari and Behra crossed the line in fourth place, enveloped in a cloud of blue smoke from a burnt piston. The other Maserati finishers were Menditeguy fifth, Mieres seventh and American John Fitch with the Moss car in ninth position.

Three minor races rounded off the season, but one was to have great significance and represented the final humiliation for Maserati in a bad year. Moss with a works Maserati (deputising for Behra, who had been badly injured in a practice crash at Dundrod) won the Gold Cup at Oulton Park from Hawthorn's Ferrari-entered Lancia, Reg Hunt finished second to Jack Brabham's rear-engined Cooper-Bristol in the Formule Libre Australian Grand Prix at Port Wakefield and then came Siracusa.

Another view of the streamlined 250F that Behra drove into fourth place at Monza. (Louis Klementaski)

The Syracuse Grand Prix, run on 23 October on a difficult, roughly triangular road circuit lined for much of its length by stone walls, should have proved a Maserati benefit. Modena entered normal 250Fs for Musso, Villoresi, Luigi Piotti and American driver Carroll Shelby and the streamliner for Harry Schell. Private 250Fs were driven by Salvadori, Gould, Rosier and Volonterio (the last-named at the wheel of the ex-de Graffenried interim car). Facing Modena were two works Gordinis and two works Connaughts driven by Brooks and Leston. It was the Connaught team's first overseas outing with the B-series and they had only been lured to the toe of Italy by the promise of vastly generous starting money.

Musso and Villoresi were fastest in practice, but the new unstreamlined Connaught of young dental student Brooks was alongside them on the front row of the grid. In the opening laps of the race the works 250Fs led from Brooks, but the English driver steadily moved through the field, passing Schell and Villoresi and taking the lead from Musso. Musso fought back, went ahead again and then Brook retook the lead to stay in front for the remainder of this 70-lap race. The Maseratis of Musso, Villoresi, Gould, Schell, Shelby and Piotti took second to seventh places, with Scarlatti's ancient 2-litre Ferrari eighth.

5. 1956: Maserati Versus Ferrari

Maserati hopes were high at the start of the 1956 season, for Mercedes-Benz withdrew from racing at the end of 1955 and this meant not only that the strength of the opposition was much reduced, but there were prospects of Stirling Moss rejoining the team. Stirling Moss tried all three British contenders, BRM, Connaught and Vanwall, at Silverstone and then consulted 17 motor racing journalists, whom he entertained at the Royal Automobile Club. Already Moss was keen to drive for Maserati again and nine of the journalists agreed that he should. He returned to lead Maserati; Behra remained with the team and Perdisa made up the trio. The team was now managed by Nello Ugolini, formerly of Ferrari. All the bitterness and disappointments of 1955 were forgotten and the year got off to a superb start.

In January, Moss drove his own car to victory in the Formule Libre New Zealand Grand Prix, winning from the Ferraris of Tony Gaze and Peter Whitehead, and then flew on to compete in the Argentine races. Four 250Fs were entered in the Argentine Grand Priz for Moss, Behra, Menditeguy and Froilan Gonzalez, the Argentinian who had been a stalwart of the Ferrari team in 1954. Luigi Piotti drove a private car entered in the name of the works, Gerino Gerini appeared with 2515, entered by Scuderia Guastalla, and Mike Hawthorn, who had signed up to drive BRMs in 1956, was at the wheel of the Owen Organization 250F. Ferrari entered a strong team of Lancia-based or Lancia-derived cars for his new team leader Juan Fangio, Musso Castellotti, Collins and Gendebien. Although Moss led the race for a short while, he retired with engine trouble, and Fangio (who had taken over Musso's Lancia-Ferrari)

This view of the nose of the much rebuilt 2501 driven by Moss at Spa in 1956 shows clearly the air exit of the ducted radiator and the radiator header tank filler. It also gives a good view of the large ribbed brake drums of the 250F. (LAT)

In 1956 Stirling Moss returned to lead Maserati in their unsuccessful struggle to beat Ferrari. This photograph was taken in 1960. (David Phipps)

won the race from Behra and Hawthorn. It was much the same story in the Buenos Aires City Grand Prix (in fact held at Mendoza, about 650 miles from Buenos Aires), where Fangio won from the works 250Fs of Moss, Behra and Menditeguy.

Giulio Alfieri, who had been Maserati's chief engineer since the end of 1954, had been working on a fuel injection version of the 250F based on the Bosch system and Moss drove this, installed in new chassis 2522, in the Richmond Trophy at Goodwood on Easter Monday. The precise output of the fuel injection engine is unclear, but Alfieri has since claimed 265 bhp, which seems rather on the high side, but the torque range was more limited and Moss was none too happy with the car. In the Richmond Trophy on the Sussex circuit Archie Scott-Brown led initially with the B-Series Connaught, but ran into mechanical problems, and Moss forged ahead to win by over a minute from Salvadori with the Gilby car. The fuel injection engine was used later in April, installed in chassis 2501 for Behra to drive in the Syracuse Grand Prix. Behra, the sole works entry, retired early in the race and the Lancia-Ferraris took the first three places.

A week later Moss drove his own car to victory in the Aintree '200', taking the lead after Scott-Brown's Connaught retired because of a broken piston and Brooks's BRM fell back with brake trouble. Maserati missed the *Daily Express* Trophy at Silverstone, so Stirling Moss was free to drive a Vanwall to victory, and the fastest of

Jean Behra remained with Maserati in 1956 as number two to Moss. This photograph of Behra, at the wheel of a Gordini, was taken in 1953. (Guy Griffiths)

the private Maserati drivers, Salvadori, crashed badly at Stowe when the rear end locked up. The following day was the Naples Grand Prix, in which private owners Gould and Gerini finished second and third behind Manzon's Gordini; Ferrari had sent two Lancia-Ferraris to this race, but both retired.

Although Maserati fielded a team of four well-prepared cars at Monaco, in reality the team was sliding into chaos, having to prepare both Formula 1 and sports/racing cars, trying to satisfy the demands of the many private owners who expected the factory to look after their cars and struggling to make headway with development work. At Monaco Moss drove 2522 fitted with a 4-speed gearbox and an engine having redesigned combustion chambers and smaller 10 mm plugs, but he also had a fuel injection car as a spare. Behra drove a new car, 2521, while Perdisa was at the wheel of 2501, fitted with a right-hand throttle so that it could be taken over by Moss if necessary. There was the usual strong entry of Lancia-Ferraris, together with works cars from Vanwall, BRM (withdrawn after engine trouble in practice) and Gordini, plus four private Maseratis. Moss took the lead at the start and led throughout the 100 laps to score only the second *Grande Epreuve* victory in his career (the first had been for Mercedes at Aintree in 1955). Both the other works 250Fs finished, Behra in third place and Perdisa seventh. It was an outstanding success for Modena.

Stirling Moss ran well in the British Grand Prix at Silverstone and was holding second place until mechanical trouble intervened. (T. C. March)

Another British driver at the fore at Silverstone was Roy Salvadori with the three-year-old Gilby Engineering car. He came right through to the front, only to be eliminated by mechanical problems. (T. C. March)

Throughout the 1956 season Maserati were constantly making changes to the 250F in their efforts to beat Ferrari. At Spa Moss drove the much-rebuilt 2501, now fitted with a long tapering nose, high-sided cockpit and wrap-round perspex windscreen; the radiator was mounted nearer the front and ducted so that the hot air emerged through a slot in the bonnet and none entered the cockpit or engine compartment. Moss tried this car in practice with both fuel injection and carburettor engines and used the latter in the race. Behra drove 2521 with the 10 mm sparking plug engine used by Moss at Monaco and Perdisa drove the standard car, 2522. The team's spare car was 2523, with long nose and ducted radiator, but with the radiator header tank mounted on the bulkhead. There was talk of Mike Hawthorn driving a works 250F at this race, but it came to nothing. There were four private 250F entries, including Francesco Godia-Sales, who had just taken delivery of 2524, which was being looked after by the works.

Moss led at the start of the race, but Fangio used the greater speed of the Lancia-Ferrari to forge ahead on lap 5. Six laps later Moss abandoned 2501 at L'Eau Rouge bridge when the left-hand wheel complete with hub and brake drum detached itself. He sprinted back to the pits to take over Perdisa's car. While Stirling rejoined the race in sixth position to fight his way through the field, Behra in third place started to drop back with engine trouble. At the flag the order was the Lancia-Ferraris of Peter Collins and Paul Frère followed by Moss, Harry Schell's Vanwall, Villoresi with the Scuderia Guastalla 250F, Pilette (Lancia-Ferrari) and Behra.

Cesare Perdisa with 2501 finished seventh in the British Grand Prix — despite the driver's loathing of the Silverstone circuit. (T. C. March)

For the French Grand Prix on the very fast Reims circuit, Maserati brought along the streamlined car, now fitted with fuel injection engine, Dunlop disc brakes (with which Alfieri had been experimenting for some time) and a 4-speed gearbox. The 250F needed a 5-speed gearbox for Reims, but this could not be used with a servo. Neither this nor the streamlined Lancia-Ferrari brought along by Maranello were raced. Moss drove 2501 and Behra, Perdisa and Taruffi were entered with standard 250Fs; Perdisa's car ran with a fuel injection engine.

Once again the Maseratis lacked the sheer speed of the opposition; Lancia-Ferraris took the first three places on the grid and fourth and fifth fastest were the Vanwalls of Schell and Hawthorn (the latter released by BRM who were still plagued by mechanical problems). In the race the 250Fs were never in serious contention and the only challenge to the Lancia-Ferraris was Schell, who retired his own Vanwall, took over Hawthorn's car and came through the field to battle with the Maranello entries until the fuel injection fell apart. Moss was in a poor eighth place when the gear-lever broke and he came in to take over Perdisa's car; unfortunately the young Italian's car had a bad oil leak, the cockpit was almost awash with oil and the car had to be swabbed out before Moss was back in the race again. Peter Collins and Eugenio Castellotti took the first two places with their Lancia-Ferraris and Behra slipped into third place after Fangio made a pit stop to deal with a split fuel line. The Argentine rejoined the race to finish fourth and Moss, completely soaked by oil, was a poor fifth. For Maserati it was the nadir of their 1956 season, the result of insufficient speed and poor and hasty preparation work.

Three standard 250Fs were entered at the British Grand Prix at Silverstone for Moss, Behra and Perdisa, and these were backed up by a total of eight private entries, including the Gilby car now completely rebuilt following Salvadori's crash at the May Silverstone meeting. Apart from four works Lancia-Ferraris, the opposition included three Vanwalls, two BRMs, three Connaughts and two of the very slow Gordinis. The most impressive Maserati performers at Silverstone were Moss, inevitably, and Salvadori. Although the BRMs led away from the start, the British

Jean Behra practising at Monza with the as yet unpainted off-set car, 2526. (Publifoto)

cars were soon in trouble, and after Fangio had spun, Moss and Salvadori moved up to hold first and second places, Salvadori was driving magnificently with what was basically a three-year-old car and on this circuit at least the 250Fs had the legs of the Lancia-Ferrari opposition. It was not to last, however, for Salvadori was forced to stop at the pits to have a trailing tank-retaining strap fixed, rejoined the race and retired soon afterwards with a misfiring engine (the problem proved to be dirt in the fuel following the rebuild at Modena), while Moss stopped twice at the pits for oil and retired out on the circuit when the gearbox broke. Fangio and Collins took the first two places for Ferrari and Behra, after another steady, unspectacular race, finished third.

Maserati were slowly learning the error of their ways and as the season progressed concentrated more and more on a team of three cars prepared as well as they could manage. At the German Grand Prix at the Nürburgring Moss drove the long-nose car that he had raced at Spa, while normal 250Fs were entered for Behra and Perdisa. In addition a total of nine private Maseratis were entered — including Volonterio at the wheel of his now-ancient interim car. During the sports car race preceding the Grand Prix, Perdisa crashed his Tipo 150S Maserati and it was decided that, although apparently unhurt, he was too shaken to take part in the Grand Prix. His place was taken by Umberto Maglioli, which meant that the Scuderia Guastalla entry became a non-starter. Fangio led throughout with his Lancia-Ferrari, his team-mate Collins held second place until lap 9, when he stopped at the pits because of a split fuel line, and Moss and Behra moved up into second and third places, where they stayed until the chequered flag. Maglioli retired the third works car with steering problems.

By the Italian Grand Prix at Monza, engineer Giulio Alfieri had produced two lower, lighter and faster versions of the 250F, in an effort to make the team more competitive with the Lancia-Ferraris on the fast Monza circuit. Although the space-frame was basically similar to that of the standard cars and the suspension was unchanged, the engine was angled in the frame by five degrees to the centre-line with the nose of the crankshaft pointing towards the right-hand front corner and the line of the transmission running diagonally across the cockpit floor to a revised final drive, with the input bevel gears offset to the left. The driver's seat was mounted on the undertray alongside the prop-shaft and much lower in the car. By mounting the steering box on the main cross member behind the engine the line of the steering was lowered. There was a long, tapering nose (with detachable panels so that the cars

For once luck was on Moss's side at Monza and he scored a fine victory with 2525 after an unscheduled refuelling stop. (Publifoto)

would fit the team's transporter), the carburettor intakes were mounted in a long, tubular duct on the bonnet, there were high cockpit sides and a longer fuel tank incorporating a head fairing. These cars were numbered 2525 and 2526 and were driven by Moss and Schell, while standard 250Fs were entered for Villoresi and Maglioli (the latter again deputising for Perdisa, who was still not fit). Six private 250Fs were also entered.

Although the new cars were still not as fast as the Lancia-Ferraris and were pushed back on to the second row of the grid by the three fastest Lancia-Ferraris (Taruffi's Vanwall was also faster), tyre troubles on the Maranello cars soon let Moss into the lead ahead of Fangio (Lancia-Ferrari), Schell (Vanwall) and Collins (Lancia-Ferrari). Then Schell with the very fast Vanwall came through to take the lead from Moss and these two swapped the lead until Schell forged ahead. Rain began to fall and the Vanwall driver eased his pace, letting Moss go ahead again.

Moss seemed all set for victory on lap 45 of this 50-lap race when he ran out of fuel at the Lesmo curve and coasted towards the pits with very little prospect of arriving there. Private Maserati driver Piotti saw the stricken Maserati, quickly summed up the situation and gently nosed the works car on its way. By the time he reached the pits, Moss already had the fuel filer open, 25 litres of fuel were poured in and he rejoined the race in second place behind Musso's Lancia-Ferrari. Two laps latter the left-hand steering arm broke on Musso's car on the finishing straight, a tyre burst and it slithered across the track out of control, stopping only just short of the pit counter. Moss went on to win the race by just under six seconds from the Lancia-Ferrari shared by Collins and Fangio. After the race it was discovered that there was only about a litre of fuel left in the tank of the winning Maserati — the bottom of the tank had split, just as it had on Behra's car earlier in the race. None of the other works Maseratis finished and the highest placed private owner was Godia-Sales in fourth place behind Flockhart's Connaught.

At the end of the year Maserati shipped out two cars to compete in the Formule Libre Australian Grand Prix held on 2 December on the Albert Park circuit at Melbourne. Moss won the race with 2501, with Behra second at the wheel of 2523 powered by a 3-litre 300S sports car engine, from Peter Whitehead's Ferrari and the private 250Fs of Reg Hunt and Stan Jones.

For Maserati the 1956 season had proved less than satisfactory, even though Moss had finished second in the Drivers' Championship with 27 points to the 30 of Fangio. During the year Moss had won only one World Championship race, the cars had proved slower than the rival Lancia-Ferraris and much of the team's efforts had been ruined by abortive development work on the cars while they were being raced and the team's commitments to private owners. Maserati learned their lesson and in 1957 preparation and organization were both much improved.

6. 1957: Fangio's Fifth World Championship

For 1957 Stirling Moss joined Vanwall, and later in the season the British team was to prove the only serious opposition to Maserati. Juan Fangio had been thoroughly unhappy at Ferrari and Maserati were as happy to welcome him back to the fold as he was to rejoin the Modena team. Behra stayed with Maserati for a third consecutive season and the other works drivers were Carlos Menditeguy and Harry Schell. Because Vanwall did not enter the Argentinian races, Moss was free to drive for Maserati in the first two races of the season.

Following the experience gained with the offset cars at Monza in 1956, Giulio Alfieri produced three new team cars for 1957 that were much improved in every respect. There was a new multi-tubular chassis frame of much smaller diameter tubing (and the engine and transmission were not angled in the frame) and with reinforcement by tubular struts. Suspension and transmission were unchanged, save that one of the works cars had welded tubular wishbones instead of the usual forged members. As on the 1956 Monza cars, the steering box was mounted on the chassis frame, but there were new and even wider and stiffer brake drums.

Although there were few changes to the engine, the intake trumpets of the Weber carburettors were now enclosed in a collector box, the top of which was sealed by the bonnet. The claimed power output was now 270 bhp at 8000 rpm, although the cars could be taken as high as 8600-8700 rpm without disastrous results.

The 1957 cars had neat, sleek bodywork with a tapering nose, heavily louvred on bonnet and scuttle, and a large rounded, riveted alloy rear tank forming a small headrest. These cars were numbered 2527, 2528 and 2529.

After his pit stop early in the race, Moss chased through the field in the 1957 Argentine Grand Prix. Here he has caught Fangio who is drifting right on the limit at close to 100 mph.

The 'Dodici cilindri' made its public debut at Siracusa in 1957, but ran in practice only. This was chassis 2523. Note the large air intake and the scoops on the bonnet for the six Weber carburettors. (LAT)

While one shop of the racing department concentrated on the preparation and racing of the three works cars, another concentrated on experimental work on the spare chassis 2501 and on the development of the new V-12 engine on which work had started in 1956. This engine, which had a capacity of 2490 cc (68.7 x 56 mm), featured twin overhead camshafts per bank of cylinders driven by an elaborate train of gears from the front of the crankshaft; the fuel, water and oil pumps were also driven from the front of the crankshaft. The deep crankcase extended upwards to enclose the pressed-in cylinder liners and there were separate cylinder heads. Lubrication was dry sump. There were three Weber 35 IDM carburettors mounted between each pair of camshafts on vertical inlet ports (there was insufficient room to mount carburettors in the vee of the engine), twin plugs per cylinder, separate Marelli motorcycle-type coils for each plug and 12-point distributors mounted at the back of each inlet camshaft.

During testing the V-12, typed the 250F/T2, developed around 320 bhp at 9500 rpm and it was designed to go up to 10,000 rpm. The engine was installed in an old 250F chassis, but the drivers soon found that the lack of torque made it almost unmanageable. Testing and development work on this new design continued throughout 1957.

Maserati shipped four cars to the Argentine for the races at the beginning of 1957. In the Argentine Grand Prix the latest cars were driven by Fangio, Moss and Behra, while Menditeguy was at the wheel of 2501. Facing them was a team of six Lancia-Ferraris. It was indicative of the strides in preparation and development taken by Maserati that Fangio, Behra and Menditeguy took the first three places ahead of Harry Schell with a car entered by Scuderia Centro-Sud. On Moss's car the accelerator broke only a few hundred yards from the start and after a long pit stop he finished eighth, with the sole consolation of having set fastest lap. The Buenos Aires

Mastery of the Maserati 250F by Fangio as he drifts 2529 with immaculate precision in the French Grand Prix at Rouen. He won the race from Musso (Lancia-Ferrari). (LAT)

City Grand Prix was run on a slower combination of roads at the Autodrome in two heats.The race was held in exceptionally hot conditions, as a result of which Moss was forced to retire. Fangio and Behra took the first two places in both heats.

It was with high hopes that Maserati returned to Europe, and the first race,the non-Championship Syracuse Grand Prix, was held on 7 April. Maserati entered 2528 for Behra and 2501 for Schell. In addition they brought along the V-12 car, 2523, which was tried in practice by Behra, Schell and Scarlatti. At this race the Maserati challenge was over before the flag had fallen. Behra's car was overheating just before the start so he and Schell swapped cars, but it had not been realized that during practice Schell's car had broken its chassis. The result was that both works Maseratis retired early in the race. The Lancia-Ferraris of Collins and Musso took the first two places ahead of Moss, who had led with Vanwall for much of the race and Taruffi with 2522 entered by Scuderia Centro-Sud.

A victory for Behra followed in the Pau Grand Prix with the sole works car entered; in the absence of the works Ferraris and Vanwalls he cruised to an easy victory ahead of Schell (Centro-Sud 250F) and the Connaught of Ivor Bueb. Maserati missed the Naples race and concentrated their efforts on the first round of the World Championship at Monaco. The usual three team cars were driven by Fangio,

Juan Fangio, Maserati team-leader in 1957 and five times World Champion, seen here at Goodwood in 1953. (Guy Griffiths)

Menditeguy and Schell, but Behra was out of the team because of a road accident. In addition the team entered 2501, which was driven by Herrmann and Scarlatti in practice and the Italian, who was faster, in the race. The V-12 car was brought along for practice only; it was now fitted with a new 5-speed gearbox tried out in a sports/racing Maserati in the Mille Miglia and a modified exhaust system with two pipes per bank of cylinders terminating in megaphone ends just ahead of the rear wheels. The V-12 was still a terrible handful and there was no question of running it in the race.

The opposition was immensely strong, with a full team of four Lancia-Ferraris, Vanwalls driven by Moss and Brooks and rather less serious entries from BRM and Connaught (it was Connaught's last race before they withdrew from racing). Moss with the Vanwall led away at the start, and the race became a furious battle, with Collins (Lancia-Ferrari) narrowly holding second-place from Fangio, Brooks (Vanwall) and Hawthorn (Lancia-Ferrari). On lap 5 Moss missed his braking point at the chicane and hit the barricade. In trying to avoid him, Collins hit the barricade on the other side of the track; Fangio and Brooks slipped by the wreckage at a snail's pace and Hawthorn, arriving on the scene much too fast, over-braked to avoid Brooks's Vanwall, struck a rear wheel of the British car and slid up the tail of Collins's car. All Fangio had to do now was to keep going, for Brooks settled for a safe second place, and at the end of the 100-lap race the Argentinian maestro was over 30 seconds in front. The other three works cars retired, but American Masten Gregory brought Centro-Sud entry 2511 home in a good third place ahead of Stuart Lewis-Evans with the 'toothpaste-tube' Connaught.

In 1957 both the Dutch and Belgian Grands Prix were cancelled, so the next round in the World Championship was the French Grand Prix, held on the difficult and testing Rouen circuit. The usual three lightweight 1957 250Fs were driven by Fangio, Behra and Schell, while Menditeguy drove 2501. There was a strong Lancia-Ferrari entry, but both Moss and Brooks were unwell, so the Vanwalls were driven by Salvadori and Lewis-Evans. Fangio and Behra dominated practice and Fangio dominated the race. Musso (Lancia-Ferrari) led initially, but on lap four Fangio went ahead and, driving superbly, drifting the 250F with immense skill through Rouen's difficult bends, placing the car within inches of the kerb and progressively lowering the lap record, pulled further and further away into the distance. The Ferrari pit was convinced that Fangio was going to stop for a wheel-change (they were deluded by activity in the Maserati pits) and second-place man Musso was urged by pit signals to catch the leader. In his efforts the young Italian set another new lap record and spun at the Nouveau Monde hairpin, but Fangio did not stop and at the finish he was over 50 seconds ahead. Behra pushed his car across the line into fifth place after the engine failed and Schell was sixth, slowed by an overheating engine. Menditeguy had been driving wildly and was eliminated when, bouncing over the straw bales, he tore away the oil pipes underneath the engine and carried on until the 250F expired for lack of lubricant.

The following weekend a non-championship Formula 1 race was held on the very fast Reims circuit. Maserati decided to concentrate on preparing two of the usual cars for the European Grand Prix at Aintree and so entered a rather mixed bag, with Fangio at the wheel of a 1956 Monza car, Behra with 2501 and Schell with 2529, the car that Fangio had driven at Rouen. In addition, on the third day of practice Maserati produced two different V-12 cars. One of these was 2523, which had run in practice for the Monza 500 Miles race with a 3.5-litre V-12 sports car engine, but now of course back in 2.5-litre form. The other was a new version of the V-12 with the engine mounted in 1956 Monza chassis 2526. While Behra was at the wheel of 2526, a piston failed and so it was decided that Menditeguy should drive 2523 in the race.

Problems with the plugs. Fangio, Bertocchi and 2529 (driven by Harry Schell) at Aintree in 1957. (T. C. March)

Reims was a good pointer to the remainder of the 1957 season. Although Fangio and Behra were first and third fastest in practice, they were split on the grid by Lewis-Evans with the Vanwall. In the race Lewis-Evans made a brilliant start, pulling clear of Musso, who led Fangio. On lap 34 Lewis-Evans lost the lead because of an oil leak that was spreading over his goggles and gloves. Fangio and Behra moved up into second and third places, but on lap 57 Fangio's brakes locked up at the Thillois hairpin. He aimed the car towards the straw bales, but they hid a very solid earth bank and the Argentinian's 250F was out of the race with bent suspension and buckled nose. The finishing order was Musso, taking the Lancia-Ferrari's only win of the 1957 season, Behra and Lewis-Evans with Schell in fourth position. Although he stalled at the start, Menditeguy had a real go with the difficult V-12 and was in ninth place when a piston failed.

Jean Behra was the star of the Maserati team in the 1957 European Grand Prix at Aintree and led the race with 2528 until the engine blew. (T. C. March)

A bare week later the Formula 1 circus was in action again at Aintree and Fangio, Behra and Schell drove the usual lightweight cars, while Menditeguy was again at thet wheel of 2501. Vanwall entered three cars for Moss, Brooks and Lewis-Evans, who was now a permanent member of the team, and there were four Lancia-Ferraris for Collins, Hawthorn, Musso and Trintignant. In practice Moss was fastest and he and Brooks were either side of Behra on the grid. On this circuit the Frenchman was at the peak of his form, while, unusually, Fangio's driving seemed colourless and below his usual immaculate standard. Moss led away at the start with Behra in second place and Fangio well down the field. On lap 22 Moss pulled into the pits with the engine of his Vanwall sounding very rough and Behra assumed a lead that it looked unlikely that he would lose.

There was a tremendous battle in the opening laps of the 1957 Italian Grand Prix at Monza between Fangio (No. 2), Behra (No. 6) and the Vanwalls of Moss, Brooks and Lewis-Evans. (Publifoto)

Moss took over Brooks's Vanwall and rejoined the race in ninth place. While Moss with the sleek green car started a frantic chase through the field, the rate of attrition amongst the red of Italy was considerable. Schell was eliminated by water pump failure, Fangio retired because of engine trouble and Moss was soon in fourth place behind Behra, Hawthorn (Lancia-Ferrari) and team-mate Lewis-Evans. Just as Moss was about to pass Lewis-Evans, Behra's engine blew up, depositing bits of metal on the track, and one of these punctured a tyre of Hawthorn's Lancia-Ferrari. Moss went on to score a magnificent victory from the Lancia-Ferraris of Musso and Hawthorn. It was a bad day for Maserati, hitherto invincible in Championship races in 1957, and the sole Modena finisher was Ivor Bueb with the old Gilby Engineering car in eighth and last place.

At the German Grand Prix the usual trio of Maserati drivers appeared with the usual lightweight cars, but Menditeguy had been replaced by a Giorgio Scarlatti, a very steady and dependable driver. In addition five private Maseratis ran at the Nürburgring. In this race there were only two Vanwalls entered, but they had serious suspension and handling problems on this circuit and were never in contention. This was to prove perhaps the most famous race in Fangio's long career. The Maserati team decided to run the 250Fs in this race with the half-full tanks so that they could be driven hard throughout the race, and when they stopped to refuel, tyres could be changed if necessary. In the first 12 laps of this 22-lap race Fangio built up a lead of 28 seconds, but the pit stop was a slow one, lasting 52 seconds and to that must be added the time lost in slowing off and regaining speed after the stop. He rejoined the race in third place behind the Lancia-Ferraris of Hawthorn and Collins, with some 50 seconds to make up. Fangio failed to close the gap on the Maranello cars during the first three laps after his stop, while the car was heavy with fuel and the tyres were new. But by the end of the lap 16 the gap was down to 33 seconds, three laps later it was reduced to 13.5 seconds and at the end of lap 20 Fangio was only a couple of

Jean Behra demonstrated the very considerable potential of the latest V-12 car at Monza, but was eliminated by mechanical problems. (Publifoto)

Although soundly beaten into second place at Monza with 2529, Fangio clinched his fifth World Championship. (Publifoto)

seconds in arrears, having progressively lowered the lap record. On the next lap Fangio passed both the Ferraris and at the finish he was 3.6 seconds ahead of Hawthorn. None of the other Maserati drivers was in the picture, with Behra sixth, Schell seventh, Gregory (Scuderia Centro-Sud entry) eighth and Scarlatti ninth.

Thanks to the cancellation of the Belgian and Dutch Grands Prix, Italy was permitted a second round in the World Championship and the Pescara Grand Prix, run on a fantastic 15.9-mile circuit that combined mountain roads and a long and very fast straight, gained Championship status. The Maserati drivers and cars were as at Nürburgring, but the team also brought along the latest V-12 car, which was used in practice only. There were three Vanwalls, but only a single Lancia-Ferrari was entered for Musso to drive. Musso led initially, but Moss took the lead on the second lap. Eight laps later the Lancia-Ferrari was out of the race with a broken engine and Fangio, secure in second place, had to settle for six Championship points without any hope of challenging the British car. Schell and Gregory (an ever-improving driver) finished third and fourth. Behra was in fourth place when his engine lost all its oil because of a broken pipe.

For the Italian Grand Prix at Monza the Maserati team decided to enter the very latest V-12 car, 2531, with Behra at the wheel. This car, which featured offset transmission and long, thin exhaust tail-pipes without megaphones, had been thoroughly tested and was much more manageable. Some indication of the improvement was that Behra was fifth fastest in practice, only fractionally slower than Fangio, and he was able to support Fangio in his battle in the race with the now undoubtedly faster Vanwalls. The opening laps of the race saw a superb struggle between Fangio with 2529, Behra, Moss and Brooks. Both Brooks and Lewis-Evans were forced to make pit stops with their Vanwalls, Behra stopped at the pits for new rear tyres and fuel at the end of lap 28, rejoining the race in fifth position, and Moss was steadily pulling away from Fangio. Behra retired the 'dodici cilindri' on lap 50 with major engine problems, Schell retired his lightweight car because of an oil leak and took over 2501 from Scarlatti and Fangio fell way back after a stop for new tyres. Although Moss made a pit stop ten laps from the finish for a nearside rear tyre and oil, at the finish he was still over 40 seconds ahead. Behind the third place Lancia-Ferrari of von Trips came Gregory in fourth place with the Centro-Sud car and Schell fifth. Although Modena had been trounced by Park Royal, it had achieved everything that was desired, wins in four of the year's Championship Grands Prix and Fangio's fifth World Championship; they had also soundly trounced their rivals from Maranello.

Before the end of the season there were two minor races in which the 250Fs were well to the fore. In the Modena Grand Prix, run on the aggregate of two 40-lap heats, Behra and Schell took first and third places with works lightweight cars. The final race of the year was the Moroccan Grand Prix at Casablanca, where Behra scored a fine victory with a works lightweight car from Lewis-Evans's Vanwall with Fangio fourth (after a pit stop to sort out a buckled nose cowling), Schell fifth and Scarlatti seventh.

At the end of 1957 it seemed that Maserati would be running a full team of V-12 cars in 1958, but it was not to be. The heavy losses incurred by Maserati in running an extensive competition programme had made the Orsis consider seriously whether they could continue racing, and a final blow, the almost complete destruction of the sports car team in the Venezuelan Grand Prix at Caracas, cast the die. There would be no more works Maseratis.

7. 1958-60: The 250F in Decline

Typical of later 250F performances — Wolfgang Seidel drove this 250F for Scuderia Centro-Sud in the 1958 *Daily Express* Trophy at Silverstone, but finished at the tail of the field after mechanical problems. (T. C. March)

By the start of the 1958 season the 250F was at the end of its development life, and if Maserati had continued to field a works team it would have been with 12-cylinder cars. Even the latest lightweight versions of the 250F, described in this chapter, were no match for the Vanwalls and Ferrari Dinos that dominated racing in 1958. Alongside the rear-engined Coopers, winner of two World Championship races in 1958 and driven to victory by Jack Brabham in the 1959-60 World Championships, they looked enormous and anachronistic. In the late fifties technical development was moving at a swift pace and as races were being shortened to less than 200 miles, so the lightweight 'sprint' cars came to the fore.

For 1958 there was a change in the fuel regulations so that Grand Prix cars were restricted to running on 'Avgas' aviation fuel. It was an odd choice, but proved an acceptable compromise between the constructors who wanted free choice of fuel, and the petrol companies, who wanted a clear identification between the fuel used by the racing teams and that sold through the high street pump. This created major problems for all the constructors whose cars had been designed to run on alcohol fuels and the Maserati works had to convert all the 250Fs to Avgas for the various private owners who were to continue racing them.

At the beginning of the year Marcello Giambertone, Fangio's racing manager, hired two of the lightweight cars for Fangio and Menditeguy to drive in the Argentine Grand Prix. Although Fangio did not finally decide to retire from racing until quite late in 1958, he made no further commitments following Maserati's withdrawal from racing and ran in only a very few events during the year. Fangio led at Buenos Aires, but dropped back after a pit stop for new tyres and because of overheating to finish fourth. The race was won by Stirling Moss at the wheel of Rob Walker's diminutive 2-litre Cooper from the Ferrari Dinos of Musso and Hawthorn; it was a clear pointer to the future. Behra finished fourth with lightweight car 2527 which he had borrowed from its new owner, racing motorcyclist Ken Kavannagh. In the Buenos Aires City Grand Prix, run a fortnight later in two heats, Fangio was the winner on aggregate from Musso's Ferrari and the lightweight 250F shared by Godia-Sales and Menditeguy.

Maserati private owners supported all the minor races in force during 1958 and regular competitors included Horace Gould, Bruce Halford (still with 2514 and 2504, respectively), Scarlatti with 2529, Godia-Sales with 2528, Scuderia Centro-Sud with 2511 and 2522, Bonnier with 2524 and the Italian girl, Maria-Teresa de Filippis with 2523 rebuilt with a 6-cylinder engine. From time to time they achieved success; Bonnier, Godia-Sales and Gould took second, third and fourth places in the Syracuse Grand Prix (won by Musso's Ferrari) and Masten Gregory drove his Scuderia Centro-Sud car into third place in the *Daily Express* trophy at Silverstone. Later in the year

Juan Fangio with the 'Piccolo', 2532 alongside Stirling Moss (Vanwall) in the 1958 French Grand Prix at Reims. In his last race Fangio finished fourth. (LAT)

A view of the second 'Piccolo', 2533, before it was raced by Scuderia Buell.

Bonnier and Halford took second and third places in the Caen Grand Prix following the retirement of the works BRMs.

At Spa for the Belgian Grand Prix the familiar Maserati blue and yellow transporter made an unexpected appearance in the paddock. It disgorged a new version of the 250F, the 250F/3, which became known as the 'Piccolo'. It looked very similar to the 1957 cars, but the wheelbase was 1.5 in shorter, it was generally smaller and some 60 lb lighter and there were mechanical changes including a smaller and lighter gearbox and modified suspension. This project had been financed by Temple

Masten Gregory with the Scuderia Buell-entered 'Piccolo', 2534, in the 1958 Italian Grand Prix. Later in the race he handed the car over to Carroll Shelby. (Publifoto)

The lightweight Tec-Mec, the last of the series, completed by Valerio Colotti after he had set up his own design studio.

Buell, an American enthusiast. The 'Piccolo' did not race at Spa, although it was driven in practice by Masten Gregory, and the day after the race Stirling Moss tested it at the Nürburgring. The 'Piccolo' reappeared at the French Grand Prix at Reims, where it was entered by Scuderia Buell and driven by Juan Fangio in his last race. Thanks to Fangio's superlative driving, the 'Piccolo' proved quite competitive and Fangio was in the fight for second place until he stopped at the pits to complain about the gearbox; he rejoined the race to finish fourth behind Hawthorn (Ferrari), Moss (Vanwall) and von Trips (Ferrari).

Scuderia Buell entered the 'Piccolo' in the Portuguese Grand Prix for Carroll Shelby, who was in sixth place with only two laps to go when he spun off because of locking brakes. By the Italian Grand Prix Scuderia Buell had taken delivery of two new 'Piccolo' cars, but only one of these ran, driven by Masten Gregory. Gregory was having his first drive since a bad sports car crash at Silverstone in July and when he tired, he handed his car over to Shelby. The 'Piccolo' crossed the line in fourth place, but was excluded from the official results because, apparently, Shelby had not been passed by the scrutineers to drive the car.

During 1959 the 250Fs were right out of the picture, but there was an interesting development at the United States Grand Prix at Sebring, where Fritz d'Orey appeared with the Tec-Mec. This was a version of the 250F completed by Valerio Colotti and was much lighter and more compact than the factory cars. Colotti had taken the half-completed car and drawings with him when he left Maserati and built the car up at his own Studio Tecnica Meccanica. It gave a good idea of the way that the Maserati organisation had been thinking. At Sebring the Tec-Mec was slow in practice and it retired in the race.

Apart from a lucky third place by Gino Munaron in the Buenos Aires City Grand Prix in February, the cars were rarely seen in the more important races in 1960 and successes were nil. At the end of the year American driver Bob Drake managed to qualify 2529 for the United States Grand Prix at Riverside and drove it into 13th place. So the 250F became the only design to compete in the first and last races of the 2500 cc Formula.

During the sixties H. C. Spero with 2514 became the first driver to appear with a 250F in Vintage Sports Car Club races and they soon became a familiar and numerous sight in Historic Racing Car events. 'Replicas' have been built and certain cars have been fitted with 'replica' chassis. So popular is the model that at Silverstone in July 1985 a total of eight 250Fs competed in a VSCC race for Maseratis only.

Appendix 1: Specification of the Maserati 250F

Note: all information relates to the 1954 car, except where indicated.

Engine: 6-cylinder in-line front-mounted 2493 cc (84×75 mm) with twin overhead camshafts driven from the nose of the crankshaft by a train of spur gears. Aluminium-alloy cylinder block and crankcase with steel liners. Dry sump lubrication. Detachable aluminium-alloy cylinder head with two valves and two 14 mm plugs per cylinder. Ignition by two Marelli magnetos driven by gear train at front of engine. Carburation by three horizontal Weber twin-choke 42 DCO3 carburettors. Power output 240 bhp at 7200 rpm (claimed), subsequently increased to 270 bhp at 8000 rpm.

Transmission: Clutch: dry multi-plate. *Gearbox:* 4-speed and reverse constant-mesh in unit with the final drive (5-speed and reverse adopted in 1955). *Final drive:* straight-cut pinion and gears, ZF limited slip differential, universally jointed drive-shafts to rear wheels.

Chassis: Frame: welded multi-tubular 'space-frame' constructed from small-diameter tubing. *Front suspension:* unequal-length double wishbones, coil springs, Houdaille vane-type shock absorbers and anti-roll bar. *Rear suspension:* de Dion axle with tube running in front of gearbox/final drive unit and located by central sliding guide and twin forward-facing radius arms on each side running to the chassis frame; transverse leaf spring running above rear axle and Houdaille vane-type shock absorbers. *Steering:* worm and sector box mounted on clutch housing behind engine. *Brakes:* two-leading shoe hydraulic in 13.4-in light alloy drums with shrunk-in steel liners and transverse cooling fins. *Wheels:* Borrani alloy-rim wire spoke 16-in with Rudge-Whitworth centre-lock splined hubs. *Fuel capacity:* 44-gallon tank in tail and supplementary 5-gallon tank mounted between gear-lever and control pedals. *Body:* aluminium panels on tubular framework.

Dimensions: Wheelbase: 7 ft 5.75 in. *Front track:* 4 ft 3.2 in. *Rear track:* 4 ft 1.2 in. *Ground clearance:* 4.3 in (approx). *Dry weight:* 1389 lb.

Appendix 2: Racing Successes of the 250F, 1954-60

* indicates interim car with 250F engine in A6GCM chassis.

Date	Race	Driver	Car	Result
1954				
17 January	Argentine GP, Buenos Aires, 3 Hours	J. M. Fangio	2505	1st, 70.13 mph
31 January	Buenos Aires City GP, Buenos Aires, 190 miles	R. Mieres	2501*	2nd
11 April	Syracuse GP, Siracusa, 268 miles	S. Mantovani	2502	3rd
19 April	Pau GP, 3 Hours	R. Mieres	2501*	3rd
19 April	Lavant Cup, Goodwood, 17 miles	R. F. Salvadori	2507	2nd
19 April	Chichester Cup, Goodwood, 17 miles	R. F. Salvadori	2507	2nd
29 May	Aintree '200', 100-mile final	S. Moss	2508	1st, 77.70 mph
6 June	Rome GP, Castelfusano, 212 miles	O. Marimon H. Schell S. Mantovani	2506 2503* 2502	1st, 102.96 mph 2nd 3rd
6 June	GP des Frontières, Chimay, 153 miles	'B. Bira'	2504	1st, 98.19 mph
20 June	Belgian GP, Spa-Franchorchamps, 315 miles	J. M. Fangio S. Moss	2505 2508	1st, 115.08 mph 3rd
11 July	Rouen GP, 301 miles	'B. Bira' R. F. Salvadori	2504* 2507	2nd 3rd
17 July	British GP, Silverstone, 263 miles	O. Marimon	2506	3rd
25 July	Caen GP, 131 miles	S. Moss	2508	2nd
7 August	Gold Cup race, Oulton Park, 100 miles	S. Moss	2506	1st, 83.48 mph
7 August	Formula Libre race, Oulton Park, 55 miles	S. Moss	2506	1st, 82.91 mph

Date	Race	Driver	Car	Result
15 August	Pescara GP, 257 miles	L. Musso 'B. Bira'	2505 2504	1st, 86.68 mph 2nd
12 September	Cadours GP, 75-mile final	L. Rosier	2506	3rd
25 September	Goodwood Trophy Goodwood, 50 miles	S. Moss R. F. Salvadori	2508 2507	1st, 91.49 mph 3rd
25 September	Woodcote Cup, Goodwood, 24 miles	S. Moss	2508	3rd
2 October	*Daily Telegraph* Trophy, Aintree, 51 miles	S. Moss H. Schell	2508 2503*	1st, 85.43 mph 3rd
2 October	Formule Libre race, Aintree, 51 miles	S. Moss S. Mantovani	2508 2514	1st, 85.26 mph 2nd
24 October	Spanish GP, Pedralbes, 314 miles	L. Musso	2514	2nd

1955

Date	Race	Driver	Car	Result
8 January	New Zealand GP, Ardmore, 204 miles	'B. Bira'	2504	1st, 78.85 mph
27 March	Turin GP, Valentino Park, 235 miles	R. Mieres	2512	2nd
11 April	Pau GP, 189 miles	J. Behra R. Mieres	2516 2515	1st, 62.34 mph 3rd
11 April	Chichester Cup, Goodwood, 17 miles	R. F. Salvadori S. Moss	2507 2508	2nd 3rd
11 April	Richmond Trophy, Goodwood, 50 miles	R. F. Salvadori	2507	1st, 89.26 mph
24 April	Bordeaux GP, 188 miles	J. Behra L. Musso R. Mieres	2516 2501 2515	1st, 64.65 mph 2nd 3rd
7 May	*Daily Express* Trophy, Silverstone, 176 miles	P. J. Collins R. F. Salvadori 'B. Bira'	2509 2507 2504	1st, 95.94 mph 2nd 3rd
8 May	Naples GP, Posillipo, 153 miles	L. Musso	2501	2nd
22 May	Monaco GP, Monte Carlo, 195 miles	J. Behra/ C. Perdisa	2512	2nd

Date	Race	Driver	Car	Result
29 May	Albi GP, Les Plânques, 194 Miles	A. Simon L. Rosier H. H. Gould	2505 2506 2504	1st, 81.60 mph 2nd 3rd
19 June	Dutch GP, Zandvoort, 260 miles	L. Musso	2501	3rd
30 July	International Trophy, Crystal Palace 21-mile final	J. M. Hawthorn R. F. Salvadori	2508 2507	1st, 77.30 mph 3rd
1 August	Rochester Cup, Brands Hatch, 37 miles	R. F. Salvadori	2507	3rd
6 August	*Daily Record* Trophy, Charterhall, 40 miles	F. R. Gerard H. H. Gould L. Rosier	2508 2504 2506	1st, 83.29 mph 2nd 3rd
13 August	Redex Trophy, Snetterton, 68 miles	S. Moss	2508	3rd
13 August	Formule Libre race, Snetterton, 68 miles	R. F. Salvadori	2507	2nd
3 September	*Daily Telegraph* Trophy, Aintree, 51 miles	R. F. Salvadori	2507	1st, 83.72 mph
3 September	Formule Libre race, Aintree, 51 miles	R. F. Salvadori	2507	2nd
24 September	Gold Cup race, Oulton Park, 150 miles	S. Moss	2516	1st, 85.94 mph
1 October	Avon Trophy, Castle Combe, 101 miles	H. H. Gould	2514	2nd
10 October	Australian GP, Port Wakefield, 104 miles	R. Hunt	2516	2nd
23 October	Syracuse GP, Siracusa, 239 miles	L. Musso L. Villoresi	2501 2516	2nd 3rd

(Note: Although the car driven by Moss at Oulton Park in September and by Villoresi at Siracusa the following month bore the number 2516, that car had already been exported to Australia for Reg Hunt.)

1956

Date	Race	Driver	Car	Result
7 January	New Zealand GP, Ardmore, 204 miles	S. Moss	2508	1st, 78.90 mph

Date	Race	Driver	Car	Result
22 January	Argentine GP, Buenos Aires, 3 hours	J. Behra J. M. Hawthorn	2501 2509	2nd 3rd
31 January	South Pacific Championship, Orange, NSW, 100 miles	R. Hunt	2516	1st, 97.40 mph
5 February	Buenos Aires City GP, Mendoza, 156 miles	S. Moss J. Behra	2520 2501	2nd 3rd
11 February	Fishermans Bend Trophy, Victoria	R. Hunt	2516	1st, —
2 April	Bathurst 100, Mount Panorama, NSW, 101 miles	R. Hunt	2516	2nd
2 April	Richmond Trophy, Goodwood 73 miles	S. Moss R. F. Salvadori	2522 2507	1st, 94.35 mph 2nd
21 April	Aintree '200', Aintree, 201 miles	S. Moss J. Brabham	2508 2509	1st, 84.24 mph 3rd
6 May	Naples GP, Posillipo, 153 miles	H. Gould G. Gerini	2514 2515	2nd 3rd
13 May	Monaco GP, Monte Carlo, 195 miles	S. Moss J. Behra	2522 2521	1st, 64.94 mph 3rd
3 June	Belgian GP, Spa-Franchorchamps, 315 miles	C. Perdisa/ S. Moss	2522	3rd
23 June	Aintree '100', Aintree, 100 miles	H. Gould B. Halford	2514 2504	1st, 83.08 mph 3rd
1 July	French GP, Reims, 315 miles	J. Behra	2512	3rd
14 July	British GP, Silverstone, 296 miles	J. Behra	2521	3rd
5 August	German GP, Nürburgring, 312 miles	S. Moss J. Behra	2501 2521	2nd 3rd
26 August	Caen GP, La Prairie, 153 miles	H. Schell R. F. Salvadori	2511 2507	1st, 80.34 mph 3rd

Date	Race	Driver	Car	Result
2 September	Italian GP, Monza, 311 miles	S. Moss	2525	1st, 129.73 mph
2 December	Australian GP, Albert Park, 248 miles	S. Moss J. Behra	2501 2523	1st, 95.99 mph 2nd

1957

Date	Race	Driver	Car	Result
12 January	New Zealand GP, Ardmore, 240 miles	S. Jones	2520	3rd
13 January	Argentine GP, Buenos Aires, 3 hours	J. M. Fangio J. Behra C. Menditeguy	2527 2528 2501	1st, 80.47 mph 2nd 3rd
27 January	Buenos Aires City GP, Buenos Aires, aggregate of two 87-mile heats	J. M. Fangio J. Behra	2527 2528	1st, 73.89 mph 2nd
10 February	Fishermans Bend Trophy, Victoria, 27 miles	S. Jones	2520	2nd
16 February	Invercargill Trophy, Ryall Bush, 99 miles	H. H. Gould	2514	3rd
4 March	Australian GP, Caversham, 154 miles	S. Jones	2520	2nd
22 April	Pau GP, 188 miles	J. Behra H. Schell	2528 2522	1st, 62.80 mph 2nd
19 May	Monaco GP, Monte Carlo, 205 miles	J. M. Fangio M. Gregory	2528 2511	1st, 64.72 mph 3rd
7 July	French GP, Rouen, 313 miles	J. M. Fangio	2529	1st, 100.02 mph
14 July	Reims GP, Reims, 315 miles	J. Behra	2501	2nd
28 July	Caen GP, La Prairie, 188 miles	B. Halford	2504	3rd
4 August	German GP, Nürburgring, 312 miles	J. M. Fangio	2529	1st, 88.82 mph
18 August	Pescara GP, 289 miles	J. M. Fangio H. Schell	2529 2527	2nd 3rd

Date	Race	Driver	Car	Result
8 September	Italian GP, Monza, 311 miles	J. M. Fangio	2529	2nd
22 September	Modena GP, aggregate of two 57-mile heats	J. Behra H. Schell	2528 2529	1st,81.09 mph 3rd
27 October	Moroccan GP, Casablanca, 260 miles	J. Behra	2528	1st, 112.64 mph

1958

Date	Race	Driver	Car	Result
18 January	New Zealand GP, Ardmore, 150 miles	R. Jensen	2508	2nd
25 January	Lady Wigram Trophy, Christchurch, 150 miles	R. Jensen	2508	2nd
1 February	Dunedin Trophy, 48 miles	R. Jensen	2508	1st, 65,00 mph
2 February	Buenos Aires City GP, aggregate of two 87-mile heats	J. M. Fangio F. Godia-Sales/ C. Menditeguy	2529 2528	1st, 66.31 mph 3rd
8 February	Invercargill Trophy Teretonga Park, 60 miles	R. Jensen	2508	1st, 67.70 mph
13 April	Syracuse GP, Siracusa, 205 miles	J. Bonnier F. Godia-Sales	2524 2528	2nd 3rd
3 May	*Daily Express* Trophy, Silverstone, 146 miles	M. Gregory	2511	3rd
20 July	Caen GP, La Prairie, 188 miles	J. Bonnier B. Halford	2524 2504	2nd 3rd
30 November	Melbourne GP, Albert Park, 100 miles	D. Whiteford	2523	3rd

1959

Date	Race	Driver	Car	Result
25 July	Lime Rock race, USA, 152 miles	C. Daigh	2529	2nd

1960

Date	Race	Driver	Car	Result
30 January	Dunedin Trophy, 70 miles	J. Mansel	2508	3rd
14 February	Buenos Aires City GP, Cordoba, ₁ 149 miles	G. Munaron	2522	3rd

Appendix 3: 250F Production

2501: Originally the number of the interim A6GCM/250F driven by Roberto Mieres. Subsequently allocated to the 1955 car exhibited at the 1954 Paris Salon. Extensively raced by the works in 1956-57 and regarded as the factory development car.

2502: 1954 works car that first appeared at the Argentine Grand Prix. Later broken up.

2503: Interim A6GCM/250F driven by Harry Schell. Sold to Reg Hunt in Australia and crashed by Kevin Neal in the 1956 Australian Grand Prix. Number never allocated to a 250F.

2504: Interim A6GCM/250F driven by 'B. Bira'. Number subsequently allocated to 'B. Bira's' 250F delivered in June 1954 and interim car broken up. 2504 was sold to Horace Gould in 1955 and Bruce Halford in 1956.

2505: 1954 works car that first appeared at the Argentine Grand Prix. Sold to André Simon in 1955 and Joakim Bonnier in 1957.

2506: 1954 works car completed in June and driven by Onofre Marimon. Driven by Louis Rosier in the 1954 Italian Grand Prix and subsequently bought by him.

2508: Stirling Moss in the wet at the 1954 *Daily Express* **Trophy at Silverstone. (T. C. March)**

2504 (Bruce Halford) leads 2524 (Francesco Godia-Sales) in the 1956 British Grand Prix. (T. C. March)

2507: First 250F to be completed for a private owner and delivered to Gilby Engineering in April 1954. Painted British Racing Green and driven by Roy Salvadori, 1954-56. Later driven for Gilby by Jim Russell, Ivor Bueb and Keith Greene. Raced in Historic events by Hon. Amiel Rothschild until end of 1984 and in 1985 by Chris Drake.

2508: Delivered to Stirling Moss in time for him to drive in the Bordeaux Grand Prix in May 1954. Taken into works team and fitted with works engine. Raced by Moss as private owner 1955-56 and subsequently sold in New Zealand.

2509: Delivered to the Owen Organization in time for Ken Wharton to drive it in the 1954 French Grand Prix. Modified by the Owen Organization with Dunlop magnesium-alloy wheels and disc brakes. Driven by Peter Collins in 1955, sold to Jack Brabham in 1956 and then to Chris Amon, who raced it in New Zealand.

2510: Interim A6GCM/250F for Emmanuel de Graffenried. Subsequently sold to Ottorino Volonterio. Number never allocated to a 250F.

2511: Completed in August 1954 for Sergio Mantovani and raced by him as part of works team, although the car remained his property. Sold to Scuderia Centro-Sud and driven by Luigi Villoresi, Umberto Maglioli, Harry Schell, Emmanuel de Graffenried and Masten Gregory.

2512: Completed in August 1954 for Onofre Marimon and crashed by him at the German Grand Prix. Subsequently rebuilt and entered by the works in 1955 for Roberto Mieres and Cesare Perdisa

2513: Rolling chassis sold to G. A. Vandervell in December 1954 for design study purposes.

2514: Completed in September 1954 for Luigi Musso and retained as 1955 team car. Subsequently sold to Horace Gould and driven by H. C. Spero, was the the first 250F to appear in VSCC Historic Racing Car events.

2515: 1955 works car and in 1956 acquired by Scuderia Guastalla. Acquired by Ottorino Volonterio in 1957 and now in the Donington Collection.

2516: 1955 works car and at the end of the year sold to Australian Reg Hunt.

2517: Chassis number not allocated.

2518: Streamlined car driven by Jean Behra in the 1955 Italian Grand Prix and Harry Schell in the 1955 Syracuse Grand Prix. Appearead at Reims in 1956 with Dunlop disc brakes and subsequently destroyed in factory fire.

2519: Completed in April 1956 for Luigi Piotti, sold to Gerino Gerini in 1958 and fitted by him with high-tail body similar to that of the 'Piccolo' cars.

2511: Masten Gregory entered by Scuderia Centro-Sud on his way to fifth place in the 1957 *Daily Express* Trophy. (T. C. March)

2518: The streamlined car as it first appeared unpainted at Monza in 1955. (Corrado Millanta)

2529: Fangio drives Schell's car in practice for the 1957 European Grand Prix at Aintree. (T. C. March)

2520: Built as 1956 works car and subsequently sold to Stan Jones in Australia.

2521: 1956 works car completed in May. Later sold to John du Puy and crashed at Casablanca at the end of 1957 by Jean Lucas.

2522: 1956 works car, Moss's winning car at Monaco, and sold to Scuderia Centro-Sud in 1957.

2523: 1956 works car completed in April and using chassis 2507 from Gilby car which had been replaced during rebuild. It ran at Spa in 1956 with long, tapering nose and ducted radiator and was rebuilt with a new chassis in August 1956. It was sold in Australia at the end of the year. The original chassis was used as the basis for the first V-12 car. In 1958 it was rebuilt in 6-cylinder form for Maria-Teresa de Filippis.

2524: Delivered in June 1956 in time for Francesco Godia-Sales to drive in Belgian Grand Prix. It was sold to Joakim Bonnier for 1958.

2525: Works car with offset engine and smaller frontal area driven to victory in the 1956 Italian Grand Prix by Stirling Moss.

2526: Works car with offset engine and smaller frontal area driven in the 1956 Italian Grand Prix by Jean Behra. Driven by Fangio in the 1957 Reims Grand Prix. The chassis number was then allocated to the second V-12 car, which incorporated parts from the original 2526. For 1958 it was rebuilt as a standard 6-cylinder car with straight engine and transmission line and sold to racing motorcyclist Keith Campbell.

2527: 1957 works lightweight car driven by Fangio to victory in the Argentine and subsequently by Harry Schell. In 1958 it was bought by racing motorcyclist Ken Kavannagh.

2528: 1957 works lightweight car driven by Fangio and Behra. Driven by Carlos Menditeguy in the 1958 Argentine races and thereafter raced by Francesco Godia-Sales. In the hands of Charles Lucas became the best-known 250F in VSCC races in the late sixties.

2529: 1957 works lightweight car driven by Moss in the Argentine and by Fangio in Europe (including his wins in the French and German Grands Prix). Raced by Giorgio Scarlatti in 1958.

2530: Lightweight version of the V-12 car that first appeared in practice at the 1957 French Grand Prix at Rouen.

2531: Lightweight version of the V-12 car driven by Behra in the 1957 Italian Grand Prix.

2532: First of the 1958 'Piccolo' cars that appeared in practice at Spa and was driven by Fangio in the French Grand Prix.

2533: 'Piccolo' car for Temple Buell raced by Carroll Shelby in the 1958 Portuguese Grand Prix.

2534: 'Piccolo' car for Temple Buell raced by Masten Gregory and Carroll Shelby in the 1958 Italian Grand Prix.

2535: Number not allocated by the works, but would have gone to the Tec-Mec if completed at the factory.